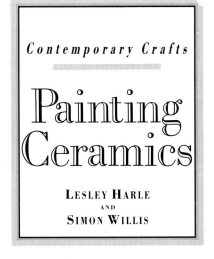

Contemporary Crafts

Painting Ceramics

LESLEY HARLE
AND
SIMON WILLIS

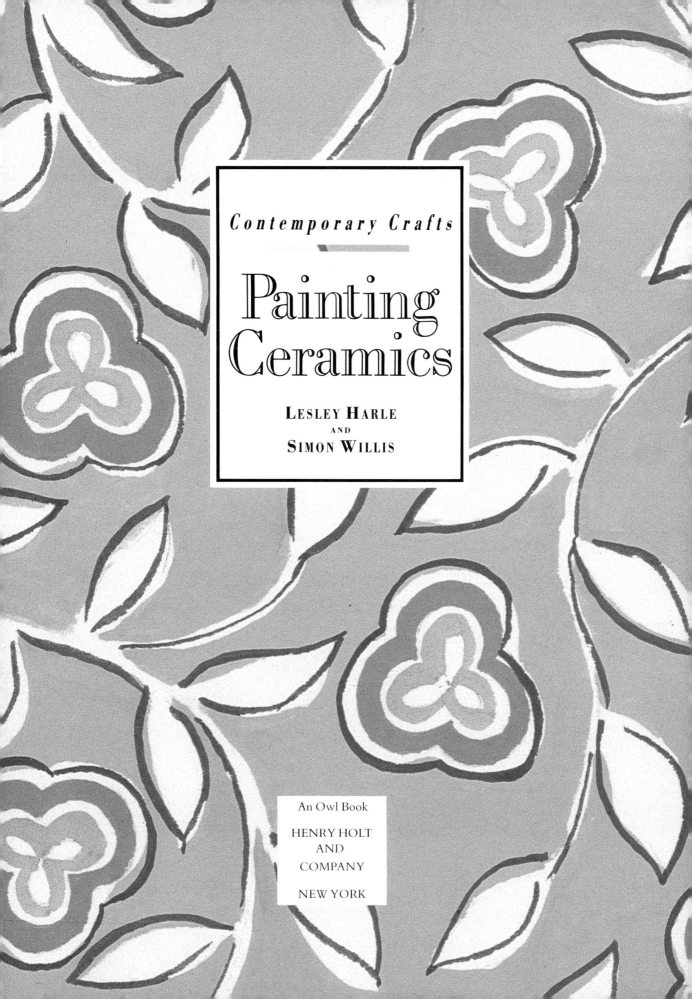

Contemporary Crafts

Painting Ceramics

LESLEY HARLE
AND
SIMON WILLIS

An Owl Book

HENRY HOLT
AND
COMPANY

NEW YORK

ACKNOWLEDGEMENTS

The authors would like to thank John Walker
for his support and help throughout.

First published in the United States in 1993 by
Henry Holt and Company, Inc., 115 West 18th Street,
New York, New York 10011.
Originally published in Great Britain in 1991 by
Charles Letts & Co. Ltd.
Letts of London House
Parkgate Road
London SW11 4NQ

Library of Congress Catalog Card Number: 92-54328

ISBN 0-8050-2383-6

Henry Holt books are available at special discounts
for bulk purchases for sales promotions, premiums,
fund-raising, or educational use. Special editions
or book excerpts can also be created to specification.

For details contact: Special Sales Director,
Henry Holt and Company, Inc., 115 West 18th Street,
New York, New York 10011.

First American/Owl Book Edition – 1993

Creative Director: Peter Bridgewater
Photographer: Zul Mukhida
Illustrator: Lorraine Harrison

Designed and edited by Anness Publishing Limited
Printed and bound in Spain by Printer Industria Grafica, S.A.

1 3 5 7 9 10 8 6 4 2

CONTENTS

The Golden Rules of Using Ceramic Paints

● This book is designed to open up the beautiful world of ceramic design to the home hobbyist and general artist. It has all the information you need on the techniques, materials and equipment required, with inspirational ideas and practical projects to set you on your way. The projects included can be created with ranges of paints and glazes that make possible firing (heat-fixing) in a domestic oven so that everything you need for ceramic design and decoration is immediately available in your home. However, care needs to be taken over the selection and use of paints and glazes, and it is very important to note the following general points:

● Regardless of advice or recommendations included in the book, you must always study carefully the manufacturer's recommendations which come with any paint products you purchase. There is a wide range of materials available, and they are constantly being refined and developed: only the producer's own literature will be fully up-to-date and accurate in its information about that specific paint-type.

● If the object created is purely for decorative use, then it is simply necessary to choose the most suitable paints and glazes for the job – there is plenty of advice in the book about what to use and when. However – and this is most important – if there is the remotest chance that the object will come into contact with food or drink, then the only *certain* way to make it totally food-safe is by designing it so that the contact area is left unpainted, or by kiln-firing it at a higher temperature than can be achieved in a domestic oven (see Kilns and Firing, page 94). Fortunately it is generally quite easy to find a local kiln – at a craft centre or pottery – that will be happy to assist in firing for a small fee, and this can be readily arranged. But if you want to stick to home-firing in the oven, then do not take any risks with anything that might come into contact with the mouth or with foodstuffs. Various ways of adapting projects such as mugs are suggested in the text and should be carefully followed.

INTRODUCTION

The word 'ceramics' derives from the Greek κέραμος, meaning potter's clay. The technique of shaping clay to form tiles, vessels and ceremonial artefacts is almost as old as civilization itself, and almost as soon as societies realized the potential of the material, they also began to decorate some of the objects they made. The projects in this book all show you how to apply decoration to mass-produced, glazed and fired ceramics, and the paints used have been developed for such application. Decoration is necessarily an aesthetic matter only, with no inherent connection between form and design. However, although the techniques need not always involve firing and the other processes traditionally associated with decorative ceramics, the development of these techniques is interesting. In looking at the forms of decoration commonly applied to ceramics, you will be able to develop and adapt the skills taught in this book to applying designs of your own to a whole range of objects.

The great attraction of buying ceramics on to which to apply decorations of your own design is that there is no need to acquire such skills as throwing a pot on a wheel, bonding pieces of clay to form handles, and so on. The corresponding disadvantage is that it precludes one of the most obvious forms of decoration – relief work. The basic texture of the object that you decorate cannot be altered using the processes described in this book.

The potter's wheel was probably invented around the fourth millenium BC in the Middle East; prior to this time and in other areas of the civilized world where clay was being used – notably China – clay objects were shaped either by building up coils of clay by hand, or by using casts. Potters had discovered that by firing the clay in kilns, the objects were strengthened,

but that an additional technique, glazing, was required in order to make the vessels non-porous. The earliest glazes used were either alkaline (made from sand fired with soda) or lead (sand fired with lead oxide). Glazes can now be bought either in a powdered form or as a glossy liquid to be applied to the surface of the clay after it has been shaped and dried, coating the clay to make it water-resistant and, in some cases, adding a layer of colour.

The very earliest painted ceramics date from the Neolithic period, when ochres and other naturally occurring pigments were used to decorate clay just as they were to decorate the walls of caves. Pottery found in the Nile valley in Egypt dates from this period and is hand-moulded; the clay was browny-red in colour, but fired to a grey finish. In Pre-Dynastic Ancient Egypt (that is, before c2686 BC), decoration normally took the forms of painted flora and fauna or of military themes. As the civilization progressed, clay came to be used to make not only vessels but also figures, generally intended for inclusion in the tombs of dignitaries and nobles, but the style of decoration remained comparatively crude.

The decorative tradition of Ancient Greek ceramics was based not on the use of coloured glazes but of oxidizing pigments, which give the familiar terracotta-and-black illustrations. In the tenth century BC, both the shape and decoration of Greek ceramics were of a stylized, geometric form that had its origins in Athens and is most characterized by the Greek key pattern. Pattern remained abstract on the whole until the appearance of the so-called 'black figure' technique – a silhouette with facial and other details incised – around 630 BC, first perfected in Corinth. The finest decoration of Greek ceramics flourished in Athens from around this time until the middle of the fifth century BC, where in addition to black-figure work, potters also developed red figures, in which the background (rather than the figures and other detailing) was filled with black.

As Rome established itself as the political and imperial power within Europe, the techniques perfected by the Greeks and inherited by the Romans were disseminated throughout Europe, as far as Byzantium in the East and England in the North. Relief decoration became prominent, as ceramics throughout this vast area adopted more or less similar techniques and results. Correspondingly, as the Empire began to wane, so too did the skills that had been learnt, and it was many centuries before European ceramics re-initiated a decorative tradition.

In the first millenium AD, the most advanced ceramics industry was in China. The history of Chinese ceramics has been the subject of many full-length books, and is impossible to cover in any depth here. The Chinese were working in ceramics in Neolithic times, and although they were using glazes from an early date, it was not until about the fourth century BC that the technique of using lead glazes was acquired. Although colour was used from the earliest times onwards, decoration of early Chinese ceramics exploited relief moulding more than painting; its subsequent development shows that applied decoration was no more important than the increasing sophistication and perfection of form. Decoration by painting received an enormous boost from the discovery and development of porcelain, the finest of ceramic materials, some time in the Tang dynasty (AD 618–906). Through trade with Persia and other Middle Eastern countries, the quality of Chinese ceramics gradually became known in North Africa and southern Europe, finally acting as one of the spurs to the rejuvenation of ceramic production in Europe as a whole.

Most pottery manufactured in medieval Europe was for use in cooking or as storage utensils, and decoration was minimal, the most notable exception being the fairly widespread use of grotesques in relief. European ceramics did not really become the objects of applied decoration until the fifteenth century, when the use of lead glazes and salt glazes was mastered. In Valencia, in Spain, large dishes were decorated with flags and coats of arms in relief work, which were then magnificently painted. A disproportionate number of such fine examples has survived, owing to the exalted use for which they were intended, but it is reasonable to assume that the development of exuberantly decorative fine ceramics was concomitant with an increase in the use of decoration on more everyday items.

By the sixteenth century, ceramic art in Europe was reaching new standards of excellence. Examples of Florentine Medici porcelain, though now rare, testify to the increasing prestige of the material; in France, at least one potter, Bernard Palissy, had established a reputation high enough to merit specific commissions from the Queen. Ceramics moved from the utilitarian to encompass the decorative: in Italy, a vogue was established for ceramic love tokens, plates painted with idealized portraits of a young man or woman, or with historical or mythological compositions.

However, it was the artists of seventeenth- and eighteenth-century Germany, collectively referred to as the *Hausmaler,* who really established ceramics as a medium as prestigious as glass, metal and perhaps even silver, producing work depicting landscapes and portraiture that ranks among the best ceramic painting ever done. It was also around this time that Oriental porcelain began to find its way on to the northern European market, spawning both a cult among collectors and a renewed interest in the quality of ceramic work, with the Meissen factory near Dresden and the Sèvres factory in France quickly recognizing the financial rewards to be reaped. The quality of porcelain was matched by an opulence of decoration. Some of the designs still manufactured today are closely related to those originally developed in the eighteenth century. The profits to be made from porcelain manufacture were no doubt helped both by the fashion for afternoon tea and by the growing ranks of an aspirant merchant class.

The development of pottery manufacture in England generally lagged behind that elsewhere in Europe. The native pottery of Tudor England was relatively plain earthenware, decorated with stained lead glazes. However, in the 1570s, two potters in Lambeth, south London, started the manufacture of pottery using majolica techniques (originally typical of Hispano-Moresque pottery in the fourteenth century, and characterized by the lustre of the glaze), which they had learnt in their native country, Holland. This style of decoration became commonly known as Delftware,

This pretty Majolica vase, made in Sweden in c.1750, is one of many historical examples of painted china that may inspire you in your own contemporary creations.

and was popular in England throughout the seventeenth and eighteenth centuries. Typical examples of London Delftware were painted using high temperature colours, usually manganese blue, green and yellow.

Objects typically decorated included drug jars, punch bowls, wine bottles, and commemorative and display plates, and in the eighteenth century, the techniques were extended to the ornamentation of tiles. Decorative themes tended to be heraldic on early pieces, but the increasing popularity of Chinese ceramic design from the middle of the seventeenth century onwards soon led to Oriental motifs, such as pagodas and lotus flowers, becoming the staple form of Delftware decoration.

Towards the end of the seventeenth century, British ceramicists latched on to a growing trend in Europe, and especially Germany, for producing stoneware with relief moulding. The most successful potter was John Dwight of Fulham, London, whose most famous work was stoneware busts of Charles II. Although the popularity of stoneware waned through the eighteenth century, Dwight's work can be seen as a direct precursor to nineteenth-century toby jugs, mugs and pitchers decorated in high relief with Bacchic scenes and grotesques.

For the most part, however, in the late eighteenth century and the nineteenth century, the demand throughout Europe and North America was for high quality porcelain. Ironically, the establishment of such great factories as Wedgwood, Spode, Limoges, Sèvres and Meissen eliminated to some extent the role of the individual potter as artist, promoting instead a consistent, standardized quality that has as much in common with mass-production as it does with art. Ceramic manufacture became a factory process, with different groups of people responsible for design, casting, firing and painting. Much fine work was, of course, produced, and different factories became particularly esteemed for different types of work: Josiah Spode II, for example, is widely credited with the discovery of the formulation of a recipe for bone china at the beginning of the nineteenth century, and this became the basis for all subsequent British table porcelain.

The return to an interest in individual craftspeople was not really reawakened until the middle of the nineteenth century, spearheaded in Britain by John Ruskin, William Morris and the Arts and Crafts Movement. In Morris's words, the aim of the Movement was to return to an aesthetic founded in the vernacular tradition, producing "art made by the people, and for the people". Ruskin, Morris and their followers insisted upon a celebration of individual talents and a rejection, to some extent, of the standardization that the industrial revolutions throughout Europe had imposed on artefacts. In addition to pottery, the Movement promoted textiles, wallpapers, furniture, metalwork and even architecture. Their objectives were taken up and re-interpreted throughout Europe and America by, among others, the Bauhaus and Frank Lloyd Wright. The legacy of the Movement lies not so much in the retrospective reproductions of many Arts and Crafts designs currently manufactured as in the vibrant craft tradition that flourishes today. In the Gallery section, the work of a number of contemporary ceramicists is showcased, illustrating the wealth, variety and individuality of designs currently being produced.

MATERIALS AND EQUIPMENT

AIRTIGHT CONTAINER
Used for storing paint you have mixed to the colour you want. Left in the open for about a day, some paints will harden to a state in which they are no longer of any use. The basic requirements of any container used to store your paints are that it is airtight and non-porous – containers that previously contained savoury spreads for sandwiches, hair gel, moisturizer and the like are ideal, provided you first wash them thoroughly. Containers made from clear glass will enable you to see what colour paint they contain; otherwise, label your jars to avoid confusion. Make sure that containers are stored out of the reach of children.

CARBON PAPER
Thin sheets of paper, one side of which is coated in carbon. Commonly used to provide a reference copy when typing letters, in the projects in this book it is used to transfer pre-drawn designs on to ceramic objects by placing the paper, carbon-side down, on to the ceramic surface and tracing round the design (*see* Basic Techniques, page 16). Carbon paper is usually dark (black, royal blue or purple), and this is what you will need when transferring designs on to white glazed ceramics. However, you can also buy white carbon paper, which you may find you need if you are transferring on to ceramics with a dark glaze.

COMPASS
An instrument that enables you to draw circles accurately and to a set radius.

MARKER PEN
A pen with a fine nib, usually used in this book to mark off points around the rim of the ceramic object. Graphic designers' pens (available from art and specialist stores) are best, since the nibs are very fine. Black ink is most suitable for marking, but try to find a pen in which the ink is not waterproof. If you have difficulty removing the marks with water, try using a small amount of neat turpentine on a clean piece of tissue.

MASKING FLUID
Usually sold as Water Colour Art Masking Fluid, this is used to mask out areas to be protected when painting, and contains rubber latex and ammonia. Make sure the surface of the ceramic is clean and dry, shake the masking fluid bottle well, and apply to the surface with a paint brush (*see* Basic Techniques, page 19). Masking fluid is toxic and should be stored away safely. Always clean the paint brush and wash your hands thoroughly immediately after use.

MASKING PAPER (FRISK)
A transparent 'film' of self-adhesive paper, with a waxed paper backing that peels away. 'Frisk' is a brand name, commonly available in art shops, although masking paper is also sold by stationery and office suppliers; another readily-available brand is 'Transpaseal'. The paper is often sold as a protective covering to be applied to book covers, maps and other documents. For the projects in this book, it is used to mask

out areas you wish to remain blank while painting.

MASKING TAPE

A self-adhesive tape, usually pale yellow, used in home decorating to protect edges around door frames, light switches and so on when painting. You can use it when decorating ceramics to keep certain areas blank while you paint others. It is particularly useful if you want to paint a hard i.e. crisp edge.

PAINT

A liquid colouring used to decorate (in this case) ceramic surfaces. The projects in this book use the following types of paint:

COLD CERAMIC PAINTS Are for decorative (*not* utilitarian) use. These are specially-formulated ranges of paints for applying to mass-produced, glazed ceramics. They are available in a range of colours and can, of course, be mixed with one another to make up other colours. **Water-based ceramic paints** have a brighter finish than solvent-based equivalents (see below), but come in a smaller range of colours. They can be diluted with water, and dry in about 4 hours. After about 24 hours, they should be hardened off in the oven as this significantly improves the durability of the decoration. Pre-heat the oven to 200°C (400°F, gas mark 6) and wait for 7 minutes if it is a gas oven, 15 minutes if electric. Place the ceramics in the oven and reduce the heat to 150°C (300°F, gas mark 2). Bake for about 30 minutes, then remove from the oven. Before baking for the first time, it is worth painting a spare ceramic tile and testing it in the oven, since various hazards should be avoided: if the temperature is too high or the ceramics are left for too long in the oven, then colours may take on a brown tinge; if the temperature is too low or the baking time is too short, however, the coloured paint will not harden; and if the paint has not been allowed to dry thoroughly before baking, the paint may bubble and blister. **Solvent-based ceramic paints** are available in the widest colour range, and can be bought with a clear glaze to 'varnish' the finished decoration, which to some extent will protect your work and add to its longevity. Solvent-based paints dry within about 24 hours of application, and can be diluted with white spirits (denatured alcohol). Cold ceramic paints can also be used to decorate unglazed

china and biscuitware but a special undercoat filler must be applied first to seal the porous surface of the china so that it does not over-absorb the colours.

ENAMEL PAINT A lead-based paint giving a smooth, hard surface covering. Commonly sold in art, craft and modelling shops, it is relatively expensive. Its lead content makes it poisonous, and obviously it is dangerous for painting any objects where there is even the slightest possibility that the item will come into contact with your own or another person's mouth. However, it is extremely durable and sold in a far greater variety of shades and colours than that of specialist ceramic paints.

CAR SPRAY PAINT Again often contains lead and/or other toxic substances, making it unsuitable for some of the projects in this book without the recommended adaptations. However, application is very quick and it is ideal for stencilling tiles: simply shake the can well and spray. Car spray paint allows you to cover large areas very quickly, it dries in minutes rather than hours, and interesting effects can be achieved by holding the can at different distances and angles to the object being covered.

PAINT BRUSH

Used for applying paint to the surface of the object being decorated. You will need a good range of sizes from fine (for applying detail) to broad (for large washes of colour). Paint brushes made from sable are the best, but they are expensive; unless you are decorating something special, they are probably not worth the extra expense. Imitation sable brushes are widely available, and are more than suitable for the projects in this book. Always clean your paint brush before applying paint of another colour and when you have finished painting; depending on the type of paint you have been using, clean the brush in either water or turpentine. Make sure that all traces of colour are cleaned from the brush, and stand it upright in a jar or container to dry.

PAINT PALETTE

An old saucer will serve the purpose, but you can also buy small, plastic rectangular trays, divided into four or five sections. For much of the time, you may be

carbon paper

airtight containers

tracing paper

watercolour paper

paints – cold ceramic, enamel, spray

paint brushes

compass

scalpel

WINSOR & NEWTON

AQUARELLE
Fluide
artistique de
masquage

AQUARELLFARBE
Maskiergummi,
flüssig

ACUARELA
Fluido para enmascarar pintura

WATER COLOUR
Art Masking
Fluid

75 ml ℮ 2.5 US fl.oz.

masking tape

pencils

masking fluid

sponge

ruler

turpentine (turps)

vert olive

Couleurs
céramique
à froid

lefranc & bourgeois

protractor

paint tray (palette)

able to use paint directly from the jar, but a palette will come in useful either when you want to mix a small quantity of colour, or when sponging paint on to the ceramic object, when the palette will allow you to control much more easily the amount of paint taken up on to the sponge or tissue.

PENCIL

Pencils are available with a range of leads, from hard to smooth. For marking ceramic surfaces, you will need a soft lead (ideally 2B), which will leave easily visible marks. However, when transferring a design using carbon paper, a hard lead (H or 2H) is more suitable, since the lead will wear down less quickly and the marks transferred will be finer and more accurate.

PROTRACTOR

A semi-circular instrument graduated with angled marks from 0–180°. A protractor enables you to measure angles accurately, and in this book is used for marking off at equal intervals the space taken up by each repeated element in a pattern.

RULER

A ruler graduated in metric on one edge and imperial on the other will prove the most useful. Metal has the advantage over wood or plastic in that the graduations are indelible and very precise.

SCALPEL (X-ACTO KNIFE)

A small, light knife shaped so that it can be held much as you would a pen, thus allowing you to cut materials very accurately. The sharp, fine blades are disposable; when one becomes blunt, only it needs replacing. Blades are sold in a variety of shapes, but the best for the purpose of the projects in this book are short and triangular in profile, with a sharp point.

SPONGE

The absorbency and texture of sponge make it an ideal material with which to achieve interesting paint effects, since unlike a paint brush it will not give an even covering.

STENCIL PAPER

Manila paper waterproofed with linseed oil, available in a range of thicknesses (gauges) from art shops. The finer the gauge of stencil paper, the easier it is to cut, and although the thicker gauges are more durable they are only really necessary if you intend to repeat your stencil design a large number of times. If you are unable to buy stencil paper, you could use acetate, although this is more expensive and more difficult to cut. A cheaper and readily available alternative is thick cartridge paper or watercolour paper, although you may have to cut a number of stencils of the same design, since repeated use will make the paper soggy.

TAPE MEASURE

It is useful to have a tape measure in addition to a ruler because of the former's flexibility, which will allow you to measure, for example, the circumference of a mug or bowl.

TISSUE

For the projects in this book, paper tissue is used for two purposes: for cleaning up areas that have been masked out, but on to which paint has seeped; and for applying paint to give a textured, 'sponged' effect. Kitchen paper tissue is generally too coarse for these purposes (although it will give an interesting, rough covering of paint), and it is best to use pieces of soft lavatory paper.

TRACING PAPER

By tracing the original design on to tracing paper, it can be transferred on to other objects by using the tracing paper in combination with carbon paper (*see* above, and Basic Techniques, page 16). The best tracing paper is sold in art and specialist shops, and is usually called artists' tracing paper.

TURPENTINE (TURPS)

A pungent liquid made from the distilled resin of certain coniferous trees. Turps is used in the manufacture of some paints and varnishes and it can be used to thin down the consistency of turps-based products. It is also useful for cleaning paint brushes after use or before you start painting in a different colour, and for cleaning areas of ceramic where paint has accidentally spilt. In some of the projects in this book, turps is also used to achieve a 'washed' paint effect (*see,* for example, the Ornamental Plate, pages 54–59, and the Fireplace Tiles, pages 40–45).

BASIC TECHNIQUES

THE PROJECTS in this book employ a variety of techniques to achieve the finished effect. While the text and photographs seek to illustrate as comprehensively as possible the stages involved in each design, you may still find it necessary to refer to this section at times. The techniques listed below will also help you to adapt your own designs for use in decorating ceramics.

WORKING OUT YOUR DESIGN

At the beginning of each of the twelve projects in the book there is an illustration of the design painted on to paper (and sometimes an alternative design, too). Obviously, this is not a stage you will have to bother with if you simply want to reproduce exactly the

designs shown, but it is still worth knowing the initial processes involved.

You should always work out your design on paper first, and in most instances it will be necessary to have the object you want to decorate in front of you. As accurately as possible, draw the shape of your vase, plate or whatever on to the paper to its actual size – since most objects are three-dimensional, you will have to imagine a cross-section drawn through the middle. You can now start drawing in the design you want to paint on to the ceramic. As you draw, think about the various components of your design and the most sensible order in which to transfer them to the ceramic object. If the design is floral, for example, it will be most sensible either to draw in stems first, and then to fit in the flowers and leaves around them, or else to drop the flower shapes at intervals around the body of the ceramic object and then fill in the leaves and stems. Similarly, think about the order of painting – if you are not very skilled with a paint brush, then try to restrict yourself to as few colours as possible and to broad areas of colour. When you have a finished design on paper, it is probably worth annotating it, or making notes to remind yourself of the order of work involved in transferring the design to the ceramic object and painting in the various elements.

Depending on how formal the design is, you may also have to work out on paper separate elements such as a border design. This may involve drawing out an overhead view of the rim of a pot (*see* Tea Service project, step 3, page 37), or alternatively measuring the circumference of the pot and drawing it out flat as a long, thin rectangle. By reading through a selection of the projects in this book, you should gain a good idea of the various pitfalls and the stages involved.

RESIZING A DESIGN

The illustrations at the beginning of each project can be used as the basis for painting the designs, but if you want to trace off the designs and then transfer them to the ceramic object then you will first have to resize them. For all of the projects in this book, this will involve enlarging the design to the correct dimensions, but you can equally use the process in reverse to reduce the size of a design.

Probably the simplest method is to use the enlargement and reduction facility on a photocopying machine, which will ensure that the design is faithfully reproduced. However, most machines only enlarge up to 156% of the original size, so you would have to use the machine twice if you wanted to double the size of the design. This method also depends, of course, on your having access to a photocopier with this facility, although an increasing number of shops now offer a photocopying service.

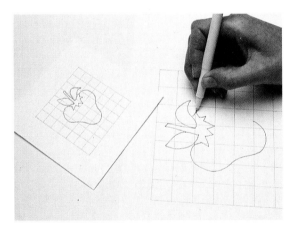

The traditional method is not difficult for most designs, although accuracy is important and you may have problems if the design is very intricate. The technique consists of drawing a grid of squares over the original design and then copying the design, square for square, on to a larger (or smaller, if you want to reduce the size) grid. First, trace the design from the book centrally on to a piece of tracing paper, transfer it on to a piece of paper and draw a grid of squares over it. On a second piece of paper, draw out a square or rectangle to the size you want the finished design and then draw in a grid of the same number of squares as are on the traced design, but larger or smaller in size (depending

on whether you want to enlarge or reduce the size of the design). Mark on the second grid the equivalent points at which the original design bisects a line on the grid you drew over it, then draw in the design on the new grid square by square, checking it carefully against the original.

For example, if you wanted to double the size of a design for one of the projects in this book, you could overlay a grid of 2.5 × 2.5cm (1 × 1in) squares on the original and then draw up a second grid of 5 × 5cm (2 × 2in) squares and then proceed as above; if you wanted to make the design half its original size, then you would simply draw a second grid of 1.2 × 1.2cm (½ × ½in) squares. The important thing is to have the same number of squares on both grids.

An interesting variation of this technique is to use it to change the proportions by distorting the original design. For example, you might have a tall, thin vase on to which you want to transfer the pansy design used to decorate the Fireplace Tiles (pages 40–45); in order to retain the sleek lines of the vase, you might decide that the design would look best if the petals were longer and thinner: draw a 2.5 × 2.5cm (1 × 1in) grid over the original design, then draw up a second grid of rectangles measuring 2.5 × 5cm (1 × 2in) so that the design remains the same width but so that the length is stretched to twice that of the original.

Always check the copied design when you have finished it against the original, drawing over the lines of the enlarged/reduced version to make sure that they are fluid and continuous.

TRANSFERRING A DESIGN

Trace the design accurately on to a piece of tracing paper cut to a size so that there is a generous margin around the design. Cut a piece of carbon paper to roughly the same size as the piece of tracing paper, and position the carbon paper, carbon-side down, on the area of the ceramic on to which you want to transfer the design. Place the piece of tracing paper on top of the piece of carbon paper, and stick it temporarily in place with a small piece of masking tape (this ensures that the paper does not slip while you are transferring the design). Now, simply draw over the traced line of the design, pressing hard with the tip of a pencil so that the carbon paper transfers the motif on to the ceramic surface. By slightly altering the position of the

carbon paper in relation to the tracing paper, you can use the same piece of paper to transfer the design as many times as you require on to the ceramic object.

MASKING OUT

It is often useful to mask out an area or areas of the ceramic object you are decorating in order to prevent paint from covering part of the surface. There are a variety of techniques you can use to achieve this, depending on the paint technique you are applying. Stencils are used not so much to mask out the blank area of the ceramic as to paint in a repeat motif represented by the outline of the stencil; masking paper, masking tape and masking fluid, on the other hand, all allow you to paint with less care than would otherwise be necessary by protecting chosen parts of the ceramic from paint.

STENCILS

Depending on the number of times you plan to use your stencil design, you can cut stencils from water-colour paper, which is relatively durable; however,

OPPOSITE: *To enlarge or reduce, draw one grid over your tracing, and make another for the new size.*

TOP: *The first stage in transferring a design is to trace off the reference material – flat artworks are presented at the opening of each project.*

ABOVE: *Transfer the design on to the ceramic using carbon paper.*

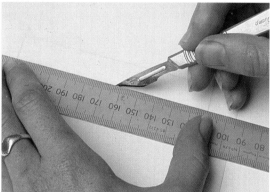

TOP: *Cut stencils accurately using a sharp scalpel (x-acto knife) and resting the work on a cutting board or mat – not ordinary wood.*

ABOVE: *Use a ruler when cutting masking paper to ensure perfectly straight lines.*

special stencil board or acetate are harder-wearing and give cleaner, more definite lines.

Cut a piece of stencil board to a size slightly larger than your motif, then transfer the motif centrally to the board using tracing paper and carbon paper (*see* above). You will need to hold the stencil on a hard, flat surface when you are cutting it out. Remember that the cutting surface will be scratched as you cut, so either buy a purpose-made cutting board or mat from an art shop or use a scrap piece of melamine (wood will quickly blunt scalpel blades and will also make accurate cutting difficult). Hold the stencil board steady and start cutting at one corner of the motif, drawing the blade in the direction of your cutting arm, *away* from your spare hand. As it becomes necessary, rotate the stencil board so that you can continue cutting with a relatively fluid movement. Always try to avoid breaking the sweep of your knife in the middle of a line, as this will probably result in a slight nick in the outline of the motif.

When you have cut out the motif (or the separate elements of the motif, if your design is more complicated than the one illustrated in the Stencilled Tiles project, page 30), you are ready to start stencilling. Tape the stencil temporarily in place with pieces of masking tape, and apply your chosen paint technique: sponging and spraying are particularly effective for stencilling, as they result in greater variation of texture.

MASKING PAPER

Cut the paper out using a scalpel. Again, consider buying a special cutting board from an art shop.

The upper surface of masking paper is difficult to mark, but you can mark the shape you want to cut out in one of two ways: mark the backing paper (which is later peeled away), bearing in mind that what you mark should be the mirror-image of the shape you want to stick down; or else mark the shape on to a piece of tracing paper and stick this down on top of the masking paper, cutting through both surfaces to leave the required design. Masking paper is very easily cut, so be careful not to rush the job. If you are cutting straight lines then it is easiest to use a ruler, ideally with a metal edge. Always hold the ruler so that the scalpel blade is on the waste side of the masking paper, so that if the blade slips you will not have to start all over again.

When you have cut out the required shape or shapes, work out their rough position on the ceramic object, then peel away the backing paper and stick down the masking paper firmly in place. Wipe over it with a soft cloth to remove any air bubbles, then run a finger nail around the edge of the masking paper to ensure that it is securely fixed. With the masking paper stuck down, it does not matter if you paint over the edges of the areas you want to keep blank. When the paint has dried to a sticky consistency, ease up one corner of the piece of masking paper using the scalpel blade and then pull it clean off the ceramic. If paint has seeped on to the area you wanted to keep blank, carefully clean it using either a fine paint brush or a small piece of tissue dipped in turps.

MASKING TAPE

If you want a hard painted edge around the border of a mug, vase or tile, then the simplest way to achieve this is by using masking tape. Simply mark at intervals the depth of the border or the width of the stripe and then carefully stick down the masking tape, aligning it with the marks. Run a finger nail around the edge of the tape to ensure that it is stuck firmly in place and then start painting.

Although masking tape allows you to paint with less care than would otherwise be necessary, you should not abandon all caution. Apply the paint so that the sweeps of your brush follow the line of the tape rather than being perpendicular to it. Do not wait for the paint to dry thoroughly before removing the tape, but allow it to dry to a sticky consistency. If necessary, wipe away any paint that has seeped underneath the masking tape.

Masking tape can also be used to mask out the tops of cups and mugs that you wish to decorate but also want to use: it is essential that paint is not applied to any areas of the ceramic object that will come into contact with your lips, unless the item is fired in a kiln (*see* page 94).

MASKING FLUID

This is most commonly used for water colour painting and allows you to mask out areas by applying the liquid to the ceramics with a paint brush. Masking fluid should be used quite thickly, and is simply applied with a brush as if it were paint. Its great advantage is

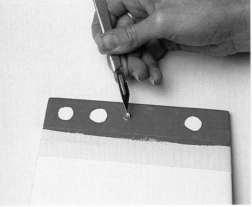

TOP AND ABOVE: *Apply masking fluid to create the shape you wish to be masked out; wait for it to dry; paint over the area to be coloured (and the masking fluid as well); then pull off the dry masking fluid with a scalpel (x-acto knife).*

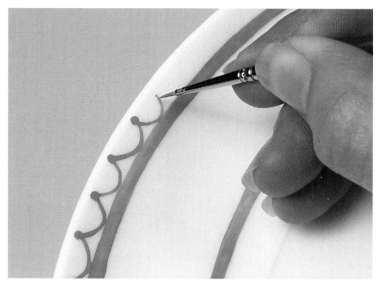

LEFT: *Keep a range of brushes suitable for delicate detail and more robust work on larger areas. Do not try to rush the work by taking too much paint on to the brush at once, or an uneven effect will be produced. Always follow the same direction once you have started a piece, so that the strokes remain even.*

BELOW: *Spray painting is one of the simplest and quickest methods, and unusual effects can be created.*

that it is so easily applied and allows you to mask out areas that would otherwise be too intricate. Simply apply the fluid to follow the shape(s) you want to mask out, wait for it to dry and then apply paint to the area you do want to cover, painting over the masking fluid as well. Whereas with the other masking-out techniques you should only wait for the paint to dry to a tacky consistency, with masking fluid you should wait for the paint to dry thoroughly. At this stage, simply pierce the dry masking fluid with the tip of the scalpel and pull it up and away from the ceramic. The rubber latex base of the fluid means that it is quite stretchy, and you may have to ease it off at the edges as you pull it away. When the masking fluid has been removed, clean up the edges with the blade to make sure you have a hard finished line. Always make sure that you wash your hands thoroughly immediately after using masking fluid.

PAINTING

PAINT BRUSH

The two most important rules when applying paint with a paint brush are firstly to match the size of the paint brush to the surface area you are covering and secondly not to take up too much paint on to your brush at any one time. Although ceramic paints are quite thick, they can be diluted using water or white spirit (depending on whether they are water-based or solvent-based); however, if you are using them for the

first time, it is worth experimenting a little first, either on a piece of paper, or ideally, on a ceramic surface such as a spare tile. Use a thick brush for covering large areas, a fine one for detail work and try to keep your brush strokes regular and following the same basic direction, whether up and down or left to right.

SPRAY PAINT

Car spray paint is extremely durable and comes in a vast range of colours, including metallics. The quality of the covering will depend on how closely you hold the can to the surface of the ceramic and the duration for which you spray. You can also achieve interesting effects by holding a 'guard' made from a piece of

cardboard against the ceramic so that you get a denser covering of paint where the spray is deflected by the guard on to the ceramic surface. Always work in a well-ventilated room when using car spray paint. You will need to protect surfaces close to where you are working with newspaper. It is worth spending a little time experimenting before actually using spray paint to decorate ceramics.

SPONGING

This will give you a dappled covering of paint and is often most effective if you apply two coats, each of a different colour. The finished look will depend upon how much paint you take up on to the sponge and the density of the sponge itself: a large, open sponge will give a broad covering, whereas a finer sponge will give a closer finish. You can also achieve a sponged look using tissue paper screwed up into a loose ball – again, the more tightly you twist the paper, the closer the finished appearance.

CARE AND MAINTENANCE

Purpose-made cold ceramic paints for the home hobbyist are non-toxic and therefore safe for general use. However, they do not conform to food safety regulations, and should on no account be used on objects that will come into contact with your mouth, nor should food be served from surfaces decorated with such paints. Ceramic paints are meant for decorative rather than utilitarian purposes and objects painted with them will not withstand repeated use unless treated with respect. Water-based paints resist scratches and are much harder wearing than solvent-based ones. Objects decorated with ceramic paints should be gently hand-washed in warm water using a mild detergent. Under no circumstances should you wash them in a dish washer, nor are you advised to soak them for too long in soapy water.

You can buy clear glaze to protect solvent-based ceramic paints – allow the paint to dry thoroughly before applying a coat. Inevitably, however, the extra protective coat will be visible and may detract from the appeal of fine paint work.

If you are decorating objects which will not be used to eat and drink from, then you need not worry about whether or not the paint is toxic. For this reason, you can use spray paint or enamel paints, which are much harder wearing. The irony, of course, is that such objects will need cleaning far less often, so ceramic paints could equally be used.

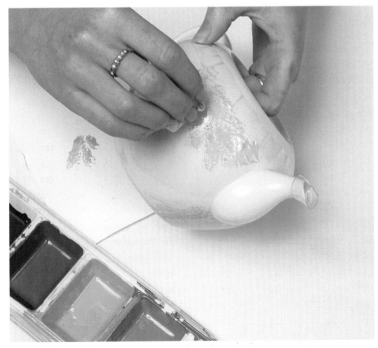

RIGHT: *Sponging has the dual advantage of allowing large areas to be covered quickly, while creating a highly attractive and interesting effect. Use different types of sponge to make the resulting dappling closer or more open – or vary your style by using tissue paper, either loosely or tightly crumpled.*

GALLERY

THE WORK featured in this section illustrates a variety of contemporary ceramic decoration. All of the artists featured are trained ceramicists, who both make and decorate their pieces, and the techniques involved are both more complicated and offer greater scope for variation than those of the projects that follow. Nonetheless, their sources of inspiration and their style of decoration could be adapted to the processes used to paint some of the projects in this book.

The diversity of styles and techniques bears testimony to the flourishing state of ceramic art today.

~

Grape Dish

ISOBEL DENNIS

Working from her own studio, Isobel produces bowls from a range of individually-crafted press-moulds that give her work a relief surface and emphasize the tactile quality of ceramics. She derives much of her inspiration from organic sources, using stylized floral and foliage designs such as the bunches of grapes illustrated here.

· · · ·

Flower Dishes

ISOBEL DENNIS

Square dish 27 × 27cm (10½ × 10½in), oval dish 20 × 25cm (8 × 10in), bowl diameter 20cm (8in)

These ceramic pieces by Isobel Dennis (see her Grape Dish for additional information) show repeated patterns on a jonquil and flower theme. As with her grape dish, these bowls reveal her love of relief and tactile surfaces, and stylized use of organic motifs.

· · · ·

Blackbird Bowl

PRU GREEN (GWILI
POTTERY)

Diameter 28.5cm (11½in)
Having gained a
scholarship at the age of
11 to Sheffield College
of Art, Pru Green began
specializing in ceramics
which led to her love
of brush and slip
techniques in
combination with resist-
glazing and stencilling.
For the past 25 years,
Pru has made her living
as a ceramicist and
decorator. She aims to
make work that is both
functional and
ornamental, and is
inspired by the idyllic
view from her studio
and pottery set in the
west Wales countryside.
. . . .

Fruit Mural

TARQUIN COLE/RYE
TILES

*Each tile 15 × 15cm
(6 × 6in)*

Tarquin founded Rye
Tiles 25 years ago,
a company now
employing about 10
people and producing
tiles for customers
ranging from royalty to
butchers. He designs a
new tile range each year
and also paints
commissioned murals:
all of the work produced
by Tarquin and his
company is to order
only, enabling
customers to select the
pattern and colours best
suited to their schemes.

· · · ·

Oval Platter

JILL BOLDING

*Length 40cm (16in),
width 25cm (10in)*

After graduating from
Brighton College of Art,
Jill Bolding spent a year
in South-east Asia before
returning to London to
work as a ceramicist.
Using one-off press
moulds and additional
spring mouldings, her
work has a tactile
quality. Inspiration is
sought from medieval
imagery and motifs, and
her particular interest is
in the combination of
form and colour.

· · · ·

Tea Pot

LISA KATZENSTEIN

Height 18cm (7in)

Lisa Katzenstein trained at the Central School of Arts and Crafts and at the Royal College of Art. Her work is inspired by the tradition of rich, classical decoration of bone china, but she seeks to inject a richness not found in insipid mass‑produced designs.

. . . .

Face Plates

KAREN DENSHAM

Diameter 36cm (14in)

Karen Densham trained in ceramics both at Wolverhampton and the Royal College of Art. The plates shown here illustrate the way in which Karen uses glazes to create a watercolour effect, with the image dissolving in and out of view. Faces and animal forms provide her with much of her inspiration for decoration.

. . . .

Marmalade Jar and Saucer

MARY ROSE YOUNG

Jar height 15cm (6in), saucer diameter 12.5cm (5in)

Mary Rose Young received a First in ceramics from Wolverhampton. She has subsequently exhibited her work widely and has been featured in a number of magazines. Her work is vibrant, with bright colours and bold designs. The use of a rose is something of a trademark in her work, the decoration in this instance combining with utility; the rose forms the handle to the lid of the jar.

. . . .

Fruit Plate

ANNIE DOHERTY

Diameter 28cm (11in)

Annie Doherty took a printed textiles course at the Middlesex Polytechnic and now works in a variety of media: painting, textiles and ceramics. Usually the source of her ceramic designs comes from one of her still-life paintings, which she then adapts to fit the shape of the ceramic piece she wishes to decorate. Annie mixes the paints herself and applies the decoration by hand, building up the design until she achieves the desired effect.

. . . .

Fruit Platter

KATE BYRNE

Diameter 40cm (16in)

Kate Byrne graduated with a first-class honours degree in 3-D design/ceramics from the Bath Academy of Art in 1984. Kate produces large one-off ceramic pieces such as jugs and teapots, as well as a limited edition studio range, of which this platter is an example. Kate likes a smooth surface for decoration, her shapes and designs being based on natural forms.

. . . .

STENCILLED TILES

STENCILLING IS ONE OF THE QUICKEST and simplest ways to decorate ceramics, and flat tiles are the easiest surface on which to apply the technique. The design shown here is very basic, and is the best project to start on if you are not confident of your skills. You could add extra interest by stencilling tiles in alternate colours or by adding a border.

MATERIALS AND EQUIPMENT

● *pencil* ● *tracing paper* ●
stencil paper or thick card or
watercolour paper ● *sponge*
or tissues ● *masking tape* ●
cold glaze ceramic paint ●
fine paint brush
. . . . . .

PREPARATION AND TIPS

● Trace off the motif from the illustration here and enlarge as necessary to fit your tile size . Transfer it centrally on to a piece of stencil paper, thick card or watercolour paper measuring the same dimensions as the tiles. If you want to stencil enough tiles to cover a wall, then it is best to use stencil paper, since this will not become soggy with repeated use. If your tiles are of different dimensions, then you will have to enlarge or reduce the design to fit (*see* Basic Techniques, page 16).

On each of the tiles that you want to stencil, mark the middle of each side and then draw a line with a pencil from the top to the bottom and from the left-hand to the right-hand side. Use these four lines as guides for centralizing the motif on the tile: the four points of the motif should align with the pencil lines drawn on the tile. With the motif centred as accurately as possible, stick the stencil to the tile using masking tape. Wipe off the pencil marks from the area to be stencilled, using a damp cloth or sponge.

1 Paint the central motif using a sponge or tissue dipped into cold glaze ceramic paint. Use a scrap of paper to remove excess paint from the sponge and begin filling in the motif. (You could use enamel paint for this project, although it would be more expensive; car spray paint is another alternative, although you would have to use acetate or special stencil paper, which lies absolutely flush against the tile.) If you want the motif to appear quite bold, you will probably have to repeat the process a second or even a third time. You may want to do this with a second colour to give a more textured effect, although you should experiment on a scrap of paper first to make sure that the two colours harmonize.

2 Work the paint into the edges of the stencil using a small piece of sponge or tissue, holding the stencil paper down with your spare hand to prevent paint seeping on to the masked-out area of the tile. Take up a small amount of paint on to a fine paint brush and very gently draw it around the outline of the stencil, being careful not to draw too obvious a line.

3 Remove the stencil from the tile, and, again using a fine paint brush, lightly dab along the edge of the motif so that it is clearly defined, but be careful to retain the sponged look. Wait for the paint to dry thoroughly, then wipe away the pencil lines that formed the 'grid'.

4 You may want to repeat the design on the corners of the tiles to create a tessellated look. Wait for the paint on the centred stencil motif to dry thoroughly, wipe away the pencil lines, and then use the edges of the tiles to line up the relevant quarter of the stencil, exactly as you did with the pencil lines. Stick the stencil in place and then apply exactly the same process as before. You can also create an attractive border along the top row of tiles by stencilling just half of the motif against one edge of the tiles.

TEA SERVICE

A COLOURFUL TEA SERVICE such as this can make a fine decorative display in a kitchen or living-room. (Cold ceramic paints are decorative and not utilitarian: if any of the items are likely to be put to use, you must not apply paint to any area that will come into contact with the mouth unless the item is fired; *see* page 94.) The elements of the design can be used in a variety of permutations to decorate each piece individually if you want. At its simplest, you can use just the sponging technique to brighten up a dull teapot. At the other extreme, you could extend the range of decorated items to plates, and you could even use enamel paints to decorate a tray to match.

~

MATERIALS AND EQUIPMENT

● ruler ● marker pen ●
Frisk masking paper ●
sponge or tissue paper ●
scrap paper ● *paint brushes*
● *cold ceramic paints* ●
compass ● *pencil* ● *tracing*
paper ● *protractor* ● *turps*
● *carbon paper*
● ● ● ● ● ●

PREPARATION AND TIPS

● Use water-based ceramic paints which are then baked in the oven for greater durability.

● Exactly the same methods as are used for the tea pot are used for the other pieces of the tea service, but in different combinations: sponging for the saucer, sponging and scallop shapes for the sugar bowl, feathers for the milk jug etc. Depending on the proportions of your service, it may be necessary to scale down the size of the motifs before applying them to objects smaller than the tea pot.

● Do not apply the scalloped border to the tea pot if you intend to serve tea from it, or paint to the edge of the tea cups.

Remove the lid from the tea pot and measure 3cm (1¼in) around the rim of the body, marking this at intervals all the way around with a fine black marker pen. Cut a strip of Frisk masking paper in a long curve, remove the backing, and stick the bottom edge of the Frisk along the line of dots.

TOP: *Using the same colours, but varying the pattern, can create an unusual and original effect.*

BOTTOM: *This is based on a 1950s design – a simple all-over pattern with bold stripes of colour.*

1 Sponge on the yellow paint to the body of the tea pot using a sponge or, better still, tissue paper. Screw up the tissue paper, dip it in to the yellow paint, and take off the excess by dabbing it on to a piece of scrap paper – this way you will get the paint to the density you want. Sponge on to the body of the pot until it is covered, working carefully around the edge of the spout, which remains unpainted. When you have finished, paint the knob on the lid of the tea pot yellow. Allow the yellow paint to dry thoroughly before removing the Frisk.

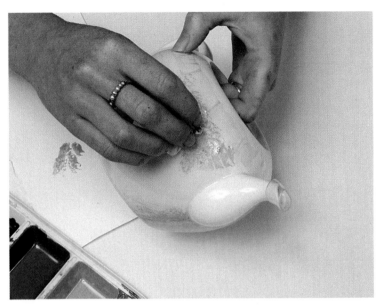

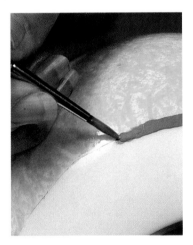

2 Remove the masking paper from around the edge of the border, and use the top edge of the yellow paint as a guide to paint in a thin green line.

3 If you intend using the tea pot, you should not apply the scalloped border, but leave it unpainted instead – miss out steps 3–6 inclusive.

The scalloped border requires time and patience if it is going to look good. Measure the diameter at the top of the body of the tea pot; halve this to find the radius, and set your compass to this measure. Draw the appropriate circle on a piece of tracing paper.

Draw another circle, concentric with the first, but with a radius 3cm (1¼in) larger – the space between the two circles represents the border at the top of the tea pot. The border of the pot is decorated with nine scallop shapes, so you need to divide the 360° circle into nine 40° 'slices' using a protractor. The area between the two circles and the outward-radiating lines is the space available for the scallop shape, which you can now draw in.

4 Trace one of the scallop shapes on to a piece of Frisk masking paper, and very carefully cut it out. Do not remove the backing paper, but instead use the section of Frisk with the scallop cut away as a template to mark off the position for the scallops around the border of the tea pot. Use a fine black pen to mark the points where the scallops join up with one another.

5 Cut a further eight pieces of masking paper with the scallop shapes traced on and then cut out. These are used to mask out the rest of the border area while you paint in the scallops. The scallops are painted in one by one, and you will need a clean piece of Frisk for each. Remove the backing from one of the pieces of Frisk and stick it down, aligning the ends of the scallop shape with the marks you have penned in. Paint in the scallop shape in green. Repeat the process, working your way around the border, but only painting every other scallop shape, since otherwise the stuck-down masking paper will smudge the scallop you have just painted. Wait for the paint to dry before painting the remaining scallops – if, as here, you have nine scallop shapes, then you will still have to wait a second time before you can paint in the final scallop. If the paint should seep underneath the masking paper, remove the excess using a fine paint brush dipped in turps.

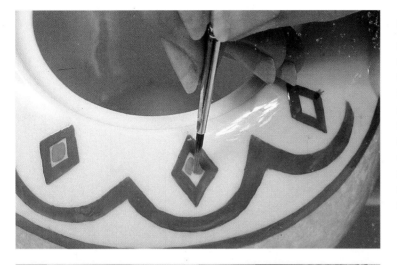

6 Return to your plan of the tea pot border (the two circles with the scallops drawn in) and draw a diamond shape the appropriate size to fit between the scallops and the top of the border. Trace the diamond shape on to a piece of tracing paper, and transfer it around the border using a piece of carbon paper. Outline the diamonds in green paint and leave to dry before filling them in with an ochre yellow.

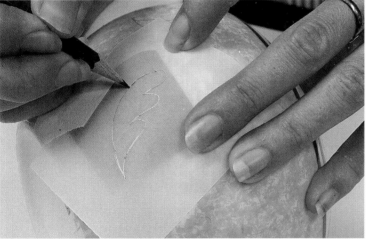

7 To complete the tea pot, draw a feather shape on to a piece of paper, and then transfer it to the yellow body of the pot using tracing paper and carbon paper. Apply the shape more or less randomly, rotating it through different angles. Paint in the feathers using one or more colours and wait to dry.

8 The cup is decorated only with the diamond shapes from the tea pot border. Transfer the shape as above, paying particular attention to spacing.

Begin with a diamond shape applied to the middle of the front of the cup – this gives you a point from which to calculate the position of the other diamonds. Calculate the spacing accurately (*see* Striped mug, page 63), or transfer a central row of diamond shapes and then fill in the rows above and below in the gaps.

FIREPLACE TILES

The design of these tiles is intended to border a fireplace. However, if you do not have a fireplace or it is unsuitable for tiling, then you could adapt the design, perhaps leaving off the border and exaggerating the twists of the stem, for other types of tile. The flower heads on their own could be used as a charming central motif on decorative plates.

MATERIALS
AND EQUIPMENT

*15 × 15cm (6 × 6in)
tiles ● tile cutters and scorer
● ruler ● pencil ● tissue
paper ● paint brushes ●
masking fluid ● masking
paper/masking tape
(optional) ● ceramic (or
enamel) paints ● scalpel
(x-acto knife) ● turps ●
tracing paper ● carbon paper
. . . . . .*

PREPARATION AND TIPS

● If your fireplace is not the height of an exact number of tiles then cut out a tile to the required size to fill the gap: score a line along the glazed side of the tile and break along this line using tile cutters. For a neat appearance, place the cut tile at the bottom of the column, where it will be hidden.

Calculate how many tiles you will need for one side of the fireplace and place them all in a row. Number them on the back from one to six, or however many tiles you need.

Measure 2.5cm (1in) in from the edge of both sides of each tile and across the top of the top tile at fairly regular intervals, marking the point with a pencil. Join up the dots using a ruler or straight edge to mark the border. Use the pencil to draw out the wavy line that runs down either side of the border and across the top. The lines drawn on either side should be approximate mirror images for a neat appearance.

LEFT: *A traditional theme and plan with autumn colours can be modernized and brightened with a splash of bright line.*

RIGHT: *A bold geometric scheme offers enormous scope: this one is coloured in the Portuguese style.*

1 Paint over the pencil wavy lines using a paint brush dipped in watercolour masking fluid, which you should apply quite thickly. Next apply small circles of masking fluid dotted at intervals between the wavy lines, for the white dots in the design.

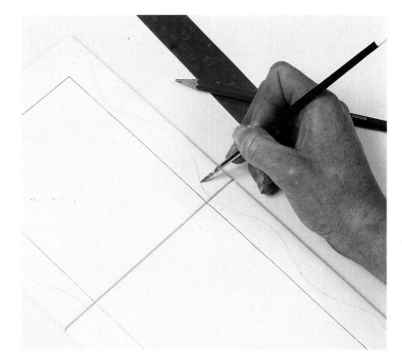

2 When the masking fluid has dried thoroughly, mix the burgundy-coloured paint from about one part blue to two parts red. If you do not want the tile to look hand-painted, then apply masking paper or masking tape along the pencilled lines of the border before you start painting, to give a hard finished edge. Apply the burgundy paint to the border, covering the entire area including the masking fluid. Be careful, however, not to paint beyond the pencil line perimeter (or masking tape) and try to apply quite a thin, even coat of paint. As soon as you have done so, apply a second coat of the burgundy colour, but more thickly this time, to give an even covering. Work as quickly as you can without sacrificing accuracy since this should prevent the brush strokes being too obvious to the naked eye.

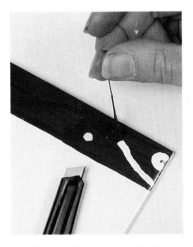

3 When the burgundy paint has dried, remove the masking fluid using the blade of a scalpel. Pierce the masking fluid towards the bottom of one of the tiles, and, using the blade of the scalpel, gently pull it up and away from the tile. Do not worry if it does not all come away in one go, or if it comes away unevenly: any that remains can be scraped away carefully. Use the scalpel to tidy the edges of the wavy line when all the masking fluid has been removed, then dip a paint brush in turps, take off the excess, and run the brush over the white line to make sure it is clean.

4 Lay the tiles out in a row again, checking the numbers on the back to make sure that they are in the correct order and that the border pattern matches up. Using a pencil, draw the sweeping central stem, curving it from one side to the other of the central area.

Draw in the smaller stems, the leaves and the pansies. You may find it easier to draw out the whole design first on a piece of paper and then use tracing paper and carbon paper to transfer it to the tiles (*see* Basic Techniques, page 16); this will also ensure that the design of the tiles on both sides of the fireplace matches up. If you do not feel capable of drawing any part of the design yourself, you could simply trace it from the illustration reproduced at the start of the project, enlarging it to fit the dimensions of your tile.

All of the central design is painted freehand, starting with the lime green stem and the leaves. If you want a flat, even finish you will have to apply two coats of the colour, just as you did with the burgundy border.

5 Once the lime green has dried, you can start to apply the darker green, first to the stem and then to the leaves. The technique used to paint the leaves is similar to that on the Ornamental Plate project (pages 54–59): apply the colour to the darkest edge of the leaf, clean your brush, and then take up a small amount of turps on to your brush and use it to spread the paint gently across the rest of the dark area of the leaf, grading the colour to give it almost the appearance of a watercolour. This effect can be quite tricky to achieve, since you want the gradation to conform to a specific scheme. Patience is called for, and you may want to experiment with the technique first on a spare tile.

6 The petals of the pansies are painted in the same way as the dark green of the leaves. Paint the yellow petals first, wait for the paint to dry thoroughly, and then paint the red. A significant part of each petal is solid colour, so be sure to apply enough paint in the first place, otherwise the pansies will look thin and washed out.

7 When the red paint has dried you can apply the black to the middle of each flower. Use a medium-sized paint brush to fill in the very centre and work around and outwards, pulling the brush in gentle strokes to give the impression of the delicate stamen.

Make sure that the tiles are thoroughly dry before fixing them in place at the sides of the fireplace. It may be a good idea to fix a temporary batten against one edge of the fireplace to ensure that the tiles are set in place exactly plumb. Take care when you come to apply tiling grout to the joints: although the excess can be simply wiped away using a damp sponge, if it is left for too long then the grout may take part of your painted decoration with it.

VASE

BLUE-AND-WHITE PAINTED CERAMICS have always been popular, perhaps the most famous being the willow pattern. The freehand design shown here updates a familiar theme, and can be as simple as you want it to be – even with just the trefoils applied, the vase already looks very attractive. This design acknowledges the fact that many people may find it difficult to paint accurately on a curved surface, and so makes a virtue of not following strictly the outlines of the trefoils, stems and leaves.

MATERIALS AND EQUIPMENT

● *cold ceramic paints* ●
paint brushes ● *pencil* ●
carbon paper ● *tracing paper*
● *masking tape*
· · · · ·

PREPARATION AND TIPS

● The first element of the design to be applied is that of the trefoils. The shape you want to apply should correspond to the main part of the trefoil, and should not include the darkest blue outline, which is applied freehand at the end. You can either draw the trefoils freehand, or you can trace off the shape from the illustration reproduced here. Look at the photograph of the finished project to get an idea about the spacing, since the trefoils need to be spaced fairly regularly in order to achieve a balanced look: you will see that the trefoils form approximate columns, running up the vase, and that they are spaced roughly mid-way between the trefoils above and below them, so that you could almost draw up an interconnecting grid of triangles. Bear in mind also that you must leave sufficient space between the trefoils to allow for the stems and leaves to be added. If you think you have pencilled in too few or too many trefoils then you will probably have to begin applying them again from scratch – the pencil marks can be simply wiped off using a damp cloth.

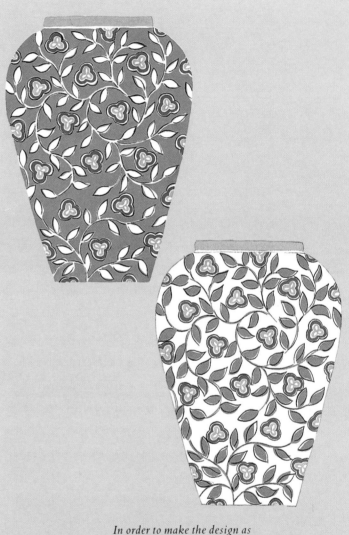

In order to make the design as successful as possible, you need to get the balance right between the three shades of blue used. The darkest blue is a neat blue used straight from a pot of ceramic paint. Rather than buy two further shades of blue, mix them by adding white ceramic paint to the original blue. When you are happy with the combination of blues (and that you have mixed enough of each to complete the project) you can start painting.

1 Paint in the blue that forms the outer band of colour (*not* the thin outline of darkest blue) and leave to dry. Paint in the yellow details: draw the brush in three petal-shaped sweeps, so that the middle of each 'petal' is left white, giving the appearance of seeds. At this stage you should also paint the rim at the top of the vase, again in yellow. Take care to try and achieve a neat finishing line between the rim and the body of the vase.

2 Make sure that the paint is thoroughly dry before proceeding, otherwise you might end up with fingerprints smudging the trefoils. Next, draw in the stems that curve between the trefoils. Try to achieve a series of main stems curving up the body of the vase, with subsidiary stems filling in any large gaps. Pencil in the curves of the stems.

Now pencil in the leaves. This is most easily done freehand, but you could trace a few leaf shapes and then transfer them using carbon paper (the danger with this method is that the masking tape used to hold the tracing and carbon paper in place may remove the pencil line of the stems and other leaf shapes when you lift it off).

3 Use the lightest blue to paint in the stems and the leaves. You will need a fine paint brush for this, and you should try to paint each sweep of the stem as one continuous stroke, since otherwise it may be too obvious at which points you started applying a fresh amount of paint. Paint in the leaves with generous sweeps of the brush.

Finally, when the pale blue paint has dried, you can paint in the dark blue outline using a fine paint brush. The pattern here depends partly for its effect on the hand-painted quality of the finished piece. For this reason, it is not important to follow exactly the lines of the trefoils, stems and leaves; the leaves benefit from the mismatch between the outline and the painted area, contributing to the loose, free quality of the design.

ASHTRAY

ALONG WITH THE STENCILLED TILES, this is the easiest decorative technique used in the book. It is also the quickest. There are really no hard and fast rules about when to stop painting, and you shouldn't have any angst about spraying as many colours down as you want. Children will undoubtedly have fun helping out, although you should always keep an eye on them, since the paint is toxic and the fumes can also be dangerous.

~

MATERIALS
AND EQUIPMENT

● *ruler* ● *compass* ● *pencil*
● *Frisk masking paper* ● *car*
spray paint ● *cardboard* ●
enamel paint ● *paint brush*
● *turps* ● *drinking straws*
. . . . . .

PREPARATION AND TIPS

● Make sure that the room you are working in is well-ventilated, as the fumes from spray paint are unhealthy and can be overwhelming.

● Cover your working surface with layers of newspaper.

● Measure the diameter of the inner circle of the ashtray (the area that you want to mask out). Halve the diameter to find the radius and set the compass to this measure, then draw out the circle on to a piece of Frisk masking paper and cut it out. Check that the piece of paper fits snugly inside the inner circle of the ashtray, and assuming that it does, remove the backing paper from the Frisk and stick it firmly down in place.

1 Take your chosen colour of car spray paint and shake the can vigorously. Before spraying on to the ashtray, experiment on a piece of paper so that you can see what effects will be achieved: obviously, the closer you bring the can of paint to the surface you want to cover, the denser the spread of colour; you can also achieve interesting effects by holding a piece of cardboard at an angle to the piece of paper (or ceramic), so that some of the spray is deflected. Once you are happy with the effects you are achieving, spray the ashtray so that you get a dappled covering of colour.

Enamel paint weathers better than the special ceramic paints used for the projects in this book – an important consideration if the ashtray is going to be subjected to everyday use. However, car spray paints and enamel paints contain lead and are mildly toxic, so you should not apply them to plates, mugs or any other objects from which you will eat or drink.

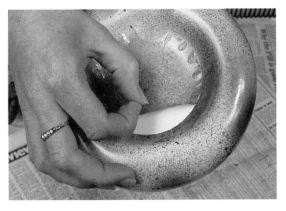

2 Enamel spray paint takes only about ten minutes to dry, so you will not have to wait long before you can peel away the masking paper from the middle of the ashtray, revealing the still-plain centre area.

3 Take the second can of car spray paint, and use the same method as before to apply your second colour, covering the whole surface. Again, wait for the paint to dry thoroughly.

4 You can splash the ashtray with as few or as many colours as you please. Bear in mind that too many colours may overwhelm.

Take a tin of enamel paint and, using a large paint brush dipped in turps, splash paint randomly over the surface of the ashtray. Really it is up to you at what stage you decide that the piece is finished. If you want to create more interesting effects than just blobs and splashes of paint, then you can blow larger drops of paint across the surface of the ashtray – blow hard through a drinking straw for maximum effect. You can create striking paint effects if you use two colours so that they begin to mix and form patterns of their own.

ORNAMENTAL PLATE

THE STUNNING washed effect on the border of this ornamental plate is more simply achieved than you would think possible. The success of the project depends little on painting skills, since the only freehand work involves the spirals on the quadrilaterals and the wavy border. You could omit these from the design if you do not have the confidence to paint them.

MATERIALS AND EQUIPMENT

● *Frisk masking paper* ●
scalpel or trimming knife ●
paint brushes ● *cold ceramic
paints (solvent-based)* ●
turps ● *cloth or tissue* ●
pencil
· · · · · ·

PREPARATION AND TIPS

● The washed effect is achieved by thinning the ceramic paints with turpentine, a technique that only works with the solvent-based variety. Make sure you buy the correct type of paint.

● The finished plate is purely for decorative use: although the decoration is durable, it will not withstand repeated washing. Obviously on no account should food ever come into contact with ceramic paint diluted with turpentine, unless the item is first fired (see page 94).

● Cut a piece of Frisk masking paper to a size that will cover the flat central section of the plate and overlap on to the raised edge. Remove the backing paper and stick the masking paper down on to the middle of the plate. Smooth the Frisk from the middle outwards to remove as many air bubbles as possible.

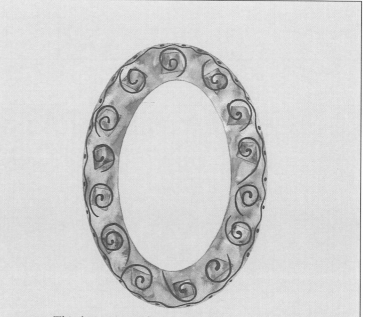

ABOVE: *This design is a modern-looking combination of graphic shapes and delicate line; the offsetting of the line over the image actually enhances the hand-designed effect and appeal, as does the deliberately variegated tone and patchiness of colour.*

· · · · · · · · · · ·

BELOW LEFT AND RIGHT: *A regular, repeated border pattern looks best on a large plate of this kind, but this can vary from a bold floral pattern (below left) to an extremely strong arrangement of structured graphic and patterned sections (below right).*

· · · · · · · · · · ·

1 Using a scalpel, carefully cut along the line of the curve of the flat oval shape to remove the excess Frisk that obscures the rimmed edge that you are going to paint. Work patiently so that the Frisk you are left with covers the oval area as accurately as possible and so that the cut line follows a smooth curve. Run a finger nail around the edge of the Frisk to seal it in place and so reduce the risk of paint seeping underneath on to the main part of the plate.

Cut the quadrilateral shapes from a piece of Frisk; although these are not regular, they should all be approximately the same size, since the design will otherwise look unbalanced. If you plan to paint the quadrilaterals in alternate colours as shown, then you must have an even number of them. You do not, of course, have to use quadrilaterals: triangles would look equally good, although shapes with five or more sides are more difficult to paint.

When you have cut out the required number of quadrilaterals – the design shown here uses 14, but the number may vary according to the size of your plate – place them in position around the rim of the plate. Do not remove the backing paper until you are satisfied that they are correctly spaced and that you do not want to change the number of quadrilaterals. When you are happy with the number and spacing, remove the backing paper and stick down the pieces of Frisk in position.

2 Mix up the colour with which you will paint the background: this aquamarine is a combination of blue and yellow. The washed effect is achieved by applying small quantities of the paint to random areas of the rim, in quite thick brush strokes.

Apply the paint to a couple of places close to one another on the plate, clean the paint brush in turpentine, and then take a small amount of turpentine on to your brush and spread the paint out from the places you have applied it. Your brush strokes do not need to be at all even, since the effect you want to achieve depends on a random combination of densely and lightly covered areas. Repeat the process until you have worked your way around the whole rim of the plate.

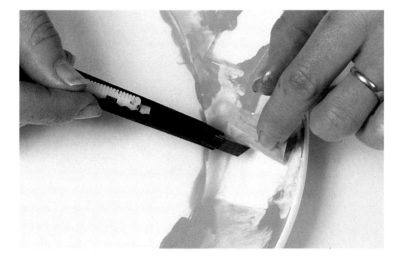

3 The paint will very quickly dry to a tacky consistency; at this stage, you can remove the pieces of masking paper. Using the edge of the scalpel, lift the edge of the masking paper and pull it away. If you find that the background colour has seeped under the masked-out areas at all, dip a piece of clean cloth or tissue in a small amount of turpentine and wipe the excess paint clean. Leave the paint to dry thoroughly.

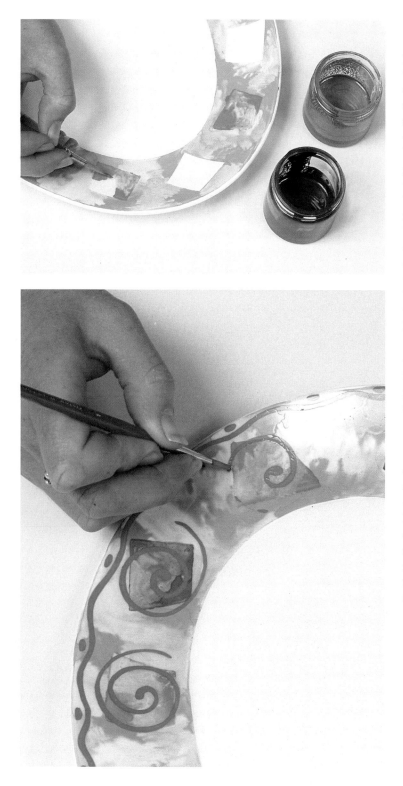

4 Paint in the quadrilaterals using exactly the same method as for painting the background. Obviously, you will need to be slightly more careful this time, since you do not want the paint to spill over on to the background colour. Use a finer paint brush and be sparing with both the amount of paint and the amount of turpentine you use. If you do paint over the background colour, wipe it away immediately using a piece of tissue. If you are right-handed, paint the quadrilaterals working in a clockwise direction, since this will reduce the risk of your hand blotching one of the quadrilaterals you have already painted; if you are left-handed, then work in an anti-clockwise direction. Paint every other quadrilateral in one colour first, wait for them to dry and then paint the remaining quadrilaterals in the second colour.

5 When the paint is thoroughly dry, apply the final touches of decoration. If you are worried about painting the spirals freehand, draw them in first using a pencil. Paint in the wavy border along the outside rim of the plate, adding spots of paint at intervals as shown in the finished photograph. Allow the paint to dry and the plate is ready.

MUGS

A SET OF brightly-painted mugs will brighten up any kitchen. Two very simple designs are described below, which should give you the basic skills to decorate as many mugs as you want, each with an individual pattern. You can buy mugs in a vast range of shapes and colours, offering even greater permutations. The mug illustrated with the elephant border gives an idea of how to expand your range as your skills improve. However, it is considerably more difficult to paint than any of the designs described overleaf, and you may want to see how easy you find it to paint freehand designs on a flat surface before trying anything quite as ambitious on a mug.

~

MATERIALS AND EQUIPMENT

● *string* ● *ruler* ● *masking tape* ● *black marker pen* ● *self-adhesive dots* ● *ceramic paints* ● *scalpel* ● *paint brushes* ● *carbon paper* ● *tracing paper*

· · · · · ·

PREPARATION AND TIPS

● Cold ceramic paints are meant for decorative and not utilitarian purposes. If you do want to use the mugs to drink from, it is important that you do not paint within the top 4cm (1½in) of the lips of the mugs, unless you intend to fire them (*see* page 94). It is a good idea to use water-based ceramic paints that are suitable for baking in the oven. If you mix colours to make up new shades, you must not mix water-based ceramic paints with solvent-based ones, unless the mugs are then fired.

Mugs offer a simple opportunity for experimentation. Floral patterns, graphic approaches, and animal devices work separately or combine equally well in any number of colours, and the above examples show only a few of the thousands of possible ideas you will be able to develop.

STRIPED MUG

1 Stick one end of a piece of string close to the rim of the mug, wrap the string around the circumference and mark the exact point at which the ends join. Remove the string from the mug, lay it down on the steel ruler – if the string will not lie flat and taut, then stick down both ends with masking tape – and measure the circumference of the mug. Decide on a convenient width for the stripes, making sure that you will have an even number of them (otherwise, you will end up with a double-width white or coloured stripe); the mug shown here has equal-width stripes. When you have calculated the spacing, mark off the intervals on the piece of string using a fine black marker pen.

2 Stick the piece of string back first on to the top rim and then on to the bottom edge of the mug and transfer the marks from the string to the mug. Obviously, the marks need to be aligned, so use the handle of the mug as a starting point: for a neat appearance, you will want a stripe to occur centrally down the handle. This will then give you a starting point from which to mark off the rest of the stripes. When you have transferred all the marks to the mug, both top and bottom, use a ruler to draw vertical lines between them.

3 Finally, paint alternate stripes in your chosen colour. The mug shown here is painted freehand, and the vertical lines are not entirely straight. If you want more accurate lines, then you could use thin strips of masking tape along the pencil lines to cover up the white areas of the mug. Whichever method you use, the only difficulty you are likely to encounter is painting the handle – do this last, and wait about four hours for the other painted stripes to dry (do not bake them in the oven yet), so that you will be able to hold the mug firmly without the risk of smudging the paint.

SPOTTED MUG

1 Self-adhesive dots are widely available from office stationers in a range of sizes. Initially, you will no doubt find large dots easier to deal with than smaller ones.

Stick the dots down firmly all over the mug, spacing them at fairly regular intervals to give a balanced look. Cut some of the dots more or less in half to stick along the bottom edge (and to the rim of the mug if it is going to be used purely for decoration or fired). You can omit dots from the handle and leave it entirely plain as shown here – these are the trickiest to paint, especially if some of them wrap around the edge of the handle on to the underside.

2 Mix the blue ceramic paint to quite a thick consistency and paint around the self-adhesive dots. Try not to cover the dots completely with the paint, as it will be easier to remove them cleanly if you just use them as a guide. When you have painted around all the circles, allow the paint to dry to a tacky consistency. At this stage, remove the self-adhesive dots using the blade of a scalpel (x-acto knife) to ease up the edge of each one, and then pull cleanly away. Leave the paint to dry thoroughly.

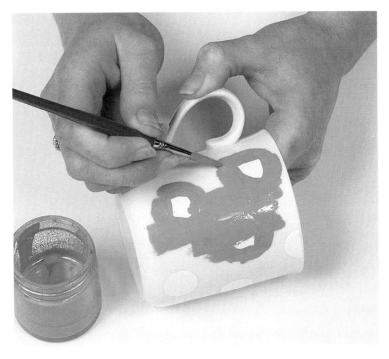

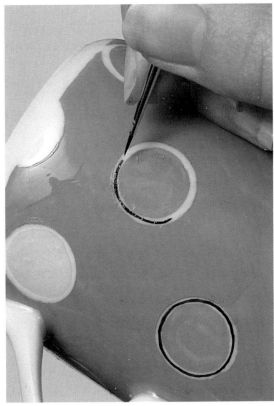

3 Mix several colours ready to paint in the spots when the blue outlines are dry. You may, of course, want to paint all the dots the same colour, but here four colours are used: pink, orange, yellow and green. Paint the spots using one colour at a time. Use the outlines left by the self-adhesive dots as a guide, but leave a thin white line between the central colour and the blue outline. Make sure that you have an even distribution of colours around the mug, so that you do not end up with, say, three or four yellow dots next to each other. Depending on your patience and dexterity, wait for each colour to dry before painting dots of a different shade, to minimize smudging.

When all the paint is thoroughly dry, paint in the outlines. Use a very fine paint brush dipped into neat black paint.

SERVING DISH

PIPING HOT VEGETABLES will look even more mouth-watering served from this beautiful dish, which is painted to reflect its contents – if you do not like carrots or mushrooms, you could easily substitute them with onions, turnips, tomatoes, peas or beans. Even if the dish you paint is oven-proof, cold ceramic paints are not, so make sure you cook the vegetables in a different dish and then simply transfer them to this dish, ready for serving. Do not apply decoration to the inside of the dish unless you intend to fire it, since, although non-toxic, cold ceramic paints must not come into contact with food or drink.

MATERIALS AND EQUIPMENT

● *black marking pen* ●
scalpel (x-acto knife), or
small scissors ● *paint*
brushes ● *ceramic paints*
(water-based)

. . . . . .

TOP: *These two approaches again*
show how very different effects can be
created from the same basic design.
Here the strong background and
graphic 'etching' devices make a
modern mood, resonant of rich
winter stews.

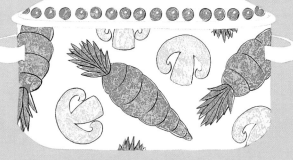

BOTTOM: *Here the much simpler use*
of sponged flat colour against a plain
background produces a lighter, more
spring-like feel. Don't be scared to
adapt any design you are using until
you find exactly the right result.

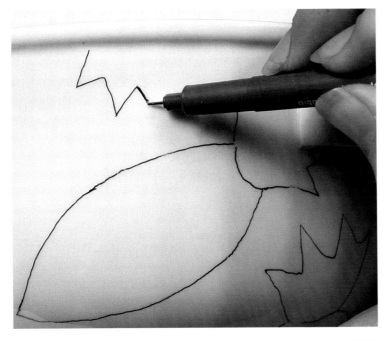

1 Decide on the vegetable shapes you want to decorate the dish – in this case, carrots and mushrooms – and draw them on to the dish with a marking pen. The shapes here are quite crude and exaggerated, so your drawing skills do not have to be great. Given this, the design will look more effective if the vegetables are drawn quite large and bold.

2 Paint the mushrooms yellow, the carrot bodies orange and the carrot heads green. The shapes are all quite large and easy to paint, so it should not be necessary to wait for one paint to dry before applying another. If you decide to err on the side of caution and paint each colour individually, then remember that the engraving must be applied before the paint is thoroughly dry.

3 Leave the paint to dry for about an hour, then start the engraving. You will need a sharp implement for this – ideally a scalpel (x-acto knife), but a small pair of scissors will suffice. Scratch away just inside the outlines of the mushrooms and carrots to suggest their gnarled surface and to give them depth. Scratching away at the paint will give different results according to how much pressure you exert on the scalpel (x-acto knife), lightening the colour of the paint in some instances, and revealing the original white ground in others. Try to get a combination for maximum effect.

4 Wait for the paint to dry, then paint the terracotta background in. Leave the handles plain (white) and use the top lip of the dish as the upper limit of the background colour, but otherwise cover all of the body of the dish. It is not important if you do not succeed in accurately outlining the mushroom and carrot shapes – it will look like additional engraving. Again, allow the paint to dry for about an hour, then use the scalpel (x-acto knife) to scratch away small spiral shapes on the background colour. Just as there is no reason why you should paint mushrooms and carrots as opposed to beans and tomatoes, so you could just as easily engrave scrolls or diamonds in spirals.

5 Outlining your work with a thin line of black paint will give it depth and definition. Wait for the terracotta colour to dry, then paint in the outlines. Use the vegetable shapes as very rough guidelines, but the outlines should be very loosely painted. Use the black paint to highlight details of the engraving, too, perhaps sweeping your brush around parts of some of the spirals and the gnarls on the carrots. Allow the black paint to dry, and the main dish is finished.

6 The lid of the dish is relatively plain. Paint the handle in the same colour as the background of the main part of the dish, and use the green paint from the carrot heads to paint a border around the edge of the lid. This can be painted freehand, using the rim of the lid as a guideline. Allow the green paint to dry for about an hour, and then scratch away roughly circular shapes in imitation of peas. When the paint is thoroughly dry, outline parts of the pea shapes in black.

FRUIT BOWL

THIS COLOURFUL fruit bowl is easier to paint than you might imagine. Although the design illustrated uses strawberries, you could just as easily choose apples, oranges, lemons, pears, bananas or any other fruit. The bowl shown here is quite large, although you could apply the fruit motifs to smaller bowls. However, in that case, it would be wise to scale down the size of the strawberries to maintain a good sense of proportion. The alternative design shown overleaf requires much greater drawing and painting skills to be tackled successfully.

PREPARATION AND TIPS

● Cold ceramic paints are not food-safe: unless you choose to take the additional precautions necessary to make your bowl food-safe, paint only on the outside of the bowl, finishing under its lip so that no fruit could come into contact with the painted area. Measure around the top rim of the bowl using a piece of string to discover the circumference (*see* Mugs project, Striped Mug stage 1, page 63). Draw a line to the length of the circumference of the bowl on to a piece of tracing paper, and then draw a second line parallel to the first – this represents the depth of the border at the top of the rim. In this design, the border represents about one-seventh of the total depth of the bowl, so you can calculate what the measurement should be for your own bowl. Having drawn out flat the area representing the bowl, draw a scroll shape on a separate piece of paper to a size that will fit comfortably within the space available. Measure the length of the scroll and calculate how many scrolls you will need for the border, taking into consideration an equal spacing of 3–6mm (⅛–¼in) between each scroll.

Use a tape measure to mark at various points on the rim of the bowl the depth of the border, then join up the points with as straight a line as possible. Next mark on the rim of the bowl the starting and finishing points of each scroll. Trace the scroll shape on to a piece of tracing paper, and, using carbon paper, transfer the scroll motif to the bowl (*see* Techniques, page 16), using the marks on the rim of the bowl and the line you have drawn in to make sure they are correctly positioned. Work your way around the rim of the bowl until all the scrolls are traced in position.

LEFT: *Although this is a strong, bold design, it is kept simple by the repetition of a single device. Leaving the background white, or using a lighter background colour, would produce a completely different effect.*

RIGHT: *Equally bold and colourful, this design is made much richer by the variety of images and the way they overlap to give the impression of superabundant fruitfulness.*

1 With the border design transferred, use a damp cloth to wipe away the spacing marks and paint in the lime green background, leaving the scroll shapes white (blank) for the time being. If you are nervous about painting around the scrolls accurately, you can mask them out using watercolour masking fluid (*see* Basic Techniques, page 19).

2 Draw or trace off and enlarge a strawberry shape from the illustration and transfer it on to the bowl. This design includes two strawberry shapes, and by using both you can add slightly more variation to your bowl. However, the most important thing is to transfer the strawberry design at approximately regular intervals and rotate the strawberries so that some are on their sides, some upside down, etc. Use portions of the strawberry shape at the edge of the border and at the base.

3 Mix a red of the appropriate shade and paint in the strawberry. It is a good idea to turn the bowl upside down and rest it on a book or similar object to give you a convenient angle at which to apply the paint, and to facilitate rotation of the bowl. Cover the whole area taken up by the body of the fruit – the small white dots are painted on later, rather than being part of the original white of the bowl. Allow the red paint to dry thoroughly.

4 Next, paint in the lime green stalks of the strawberries. When these, too, are dry, paint the dark green around the base of the bowl (if applicable), the leaves and the scrolls (remember to remove the masking fluid first if you used that method – *see* Basic Techniques, page 19). Use the dark green to paint the base first, then go back and paint the leaves and scrolls, rotating the bowl until they are all done. (If you leave the base until last, you may smudge the newly-painted scrolls as you try to turn the bowl around).

5 Wait for the dark green paint to dry. Using a fine paint brush dipped in pure white paint, apply small dots to the bodies of the strawberries.

6 Finally, use a very fine paint brush and neat black paint to outline the strawberries and the scroll shapes, and to paint in the central vein of each leaf. The design thrives on the vibrant, hand-painted look, so you do not have to apply the outlines with perfect accuracy.

BEADS

CERAMIC BEADS are available in a variety of shapes, sizes and colours. The decoration shown here relies on the subtle combination of colours for its effect, and is quite easy to do once you have mastered the knack of covering each bead with an even coat of the base colour. However, you could be more ambitious, and paint the beads in the geometrical patterns shown in the alternative design, or you could paint them in imitation of oriental beads, with small birds or lotus leaves. The painted beads can be made up into earrings, bracelets or necklaces, and it would be relatively quick and easy to make enough beads for a matching set of jewellery.

MATERIALS AND EQUIPMENT

● *cocktail sticks (or lengths of string)* ● *paint brush* ● *2 off-cuts of wood* ● *ceramic paints* ● *gold paint*

For stringing the beads:
● *pliers* ● *glue* ● *wire or nylon thread* ● *appropriate clasps or ear-fittings* ● *PVA adhesive*

. . . . . .

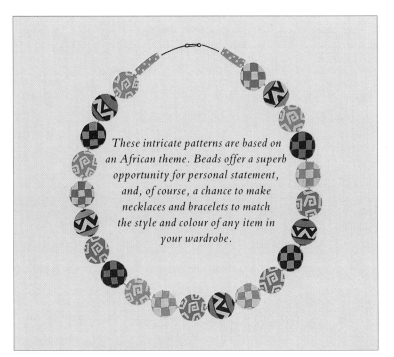

These intricate patterns are based on an African theme. Beads offer a superb opportunity for personal statement, and, of course, a chance to make necklaces and bracelets to match the style and colour of any item in your wardrobe.

PREPARATION AND TIPS

● Mix the paints to the colour or colours you want to paint the beads: the burgundy shown here is a combination of red and blue. The paint needs to be of quite a thick consistency to give a regular covering of colour. Paint the beads by dipping them in the glaze using one of two methods. Whichever method you use, you will find that the most difficult thing is to cover the bead completely and evenly. If the whole of the surface is not covered, use a paint brush to touch up the blank areas. The danger of applying too much paint is that a drip may form as it dries. If this seems likely to happen, spin the bead on the piece of string or use two cocktail sticks to rotate the bead on its axis so that a drip forms (it also helps to ensure an even covering of paint), which can be gently removed with a fine brush.

● To make up into pieces of jewellery, you can buy the necessary materials from a craft or specialist store.

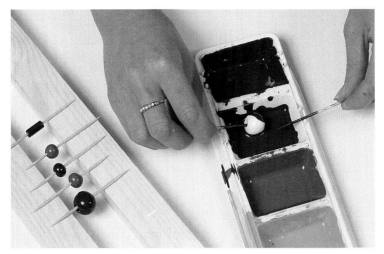

1 Cut a piece of string about 10cm (4in) long; tie a knot in one end, making sure it is large enough to prevent the bead from falling through, then dunk the bead into the pot of paint.

Alternatively, thread a cocktail stick through the bead and dip the bead into a tray of paint. Use the cocktail stick to coax the bead around the tray of paint until it is almost covered; you may find the operation easier if you use a second cocktail stick held in your other hand to roll the bead, giving you greater control, and preventing the bead from falling off the other stick.

2 Leave the beads to dry, either by hanging the unknotted end of string from the top of a shelf or convenient surface and weighting it down with a heavy object, or by resting both ends of the cocktail stick between two off-cuts of wood of equal depth placed on a flat surface. After about half an hour, check that no drips have started to form; follow the 'Preparation' procedure if they have.

3 When the ground colour has dried, the beads may be decorated with the gold paint. Place the bead on to the end of a paint brush or the sharpened end of a pencil – you should find that it will fit quite firmly, enabling you to rotate the brush or pencil with one hand as you apply the gold paint with the other. The design shown here is entirely freehand, and it does not really matter if some beads have more gold swirls on them than others. Obviously, you could use a combination of swirls, spots and other shapes, perhaps alternating the design of successive beads. Avoid taking up too much gold paint on to your paint brush at any one time, since this will hinder your ability to apply the decoration accurately and evenly. When the gold paint has been applied, leave the bead to dry, propping the paint brush or pencil in a jam jar or mug.

To make a necklace or bracelet you will not need to buy any specialist clasps or fixings. Simply cut a length of wire or nylon thread to the required length: for strength, you should thread the beads on to a double length of

thread, allowing about 5cm (2in) over. Tie a large knot in the end of the thread, and apply a drop of PVA adhesive to hold it firmly. Wait for this to dry, then start threading the beads; when they are all in place, pull them together so that the thread is taut, then tie another knot in the free end of the

thread – this should be as close to the final bead as you can make it. Finally, twist the two ends of wire together so that they make a secure joining, and cut off any excess length of thread. Apply a further dab of PVA adhesive to ensure a firm fixing and to encase the loose ends.

STORAGE JAR

LETTERING CAN BE used to personalize a variety of mass-produced ceramic objects, from initials on mugs to house names painted on plain tiles. The lettering shown here to decorate a storage jar for pasta is composed of entirely straight lines, making painting considerably simpler. Of course, there is nothing to stop you from combining the lettering with other designs, either those featured as projects in the book or something you have thought of yourself. A series of storage jars could be painted with freehand motifs to reflect their contents, or you could set the lettering within a panel and apply spots or stripes to the rest of the container, using the techniques described in the Mugs project on page 60.

MATERIALS AND EQUIPMENT

● *paint brushes* ● *tracing paper* ● *Frisk masking paper* ● *pencil* ● *ruler* ● *scalpel (x-acto knife)* ● *turps* ● *ceramic (or enamel) paints*

. . . . . .

PREPARATION AND TIPS

● The alphabet shown here will enable you to paint whatever words you wish. Each letter is decorated with a different pattern.

● If you plan to letter a group of objects – whether they are storage jars, cereal bowls or mugs – you may have to alter the size of the letters according to the length of the longest word. For example, if you wanted to paint jars to hold tea, coffee and sugar, you might have to calculate the maximum size you can paint the letters in order to fit the word 'COFFEE' on one side of the jar.

Start by tracing off the letters necessary to spell the word that you want to paint. Draw a straight line on to a piece of tracing paper and use this as a base line on which to trace the relevant letters. Use a steel ruler as you trace the letters in order to reproduce them as accurately as possible.

Cut a piece of Frisk masking paper to a size that comfortably covers the area taken up by the lettering you have traced. Place the Frisk over the tracing paper on a hard, flat cutting surface, using masking tape to stick it down firmly.

Lettering can be one of the most useful of all the decorative skills. Once you have mastered it, it can be applied not only to storage jars, but also to personalized mugs and other crockery, and, more adventurously, to commemorative plates and plaques to celebrate special occasions. The sample here shows only one alphabet to copy: thousands of others can be found in calligraphy books and in the type-face manuals used by graphic designers and printers. If the lettering patterns shown here seem too complicated, you could restrict yourself to something simple like dots or circles.

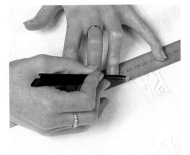

1 Start cutting out the letters using a steel ruler and a sharp scalpel (x-acto knife). On certain letters ('P' and 'A' in this example), you will also need to cut small pieces of Frisk that mask out the middle.

Measure the height of the storage line from the base to the top rim of the main part of the jar. Measure a point about half way up the jar as a base line for the lettering to sit on and mark this in three places. Join up the points to form a horizontal line. Measure the width of the front face of the jar and mark the mid point in three places; join up these points to form a vertical line. These lines will enable you to position the lettering accurately.

Carefully peel away the masking paper from the tracing paper and stick on to the storage jar using the pencil guidelines you have just drawn: the bottom edge of the lettering should sit exactly on the horizontal line and the middle letter (in this example, the 'S') should be centred on the vertical line. Firmly rub along the edges of the lettering with your finger nail to ensure that the Frisk is securely stuck down. Remember to stick in the pieces of Frisk to mask out the centres of certain letters, such as 'A', 'B', 'O' etc.

2 Start painting the letters in black, or whatever colour you have decided on. Apply the paint with some caution so that you minimize the risk of the paint seeping underneath the Frisk.

Allow the paint to dry until it is sticky (about 20 minutes) and then gently peel away the Frisk. Use a fine paint brush and turps to remove unwanted blemishes. Leave the paint to dry thoroughly.

3 When the lettering is completely dry you can apply the white decorative patterns. Use a fine paint brush and undiluted white ceramic paint or enamel paint. Each letter in the alphabet illustrated is decorated with a different pattern, and some of the designs require more skill than others to apply. You may, of course, want to leave the lettering entirely plain; alternatively, you could apply just one design to all of the letters, or just to recurring ones.

DECORATIVE PLATE

FLOWERS HAVE REMAINED an ever-popular motif in the decoration of ceramics. The design here has a delicate charm all of its own, and will make a delightful kitchen ornament, or, if kiln-fired, will lend a sense of occasion to any meal served from plates decorated with it. If you do wish to make a functional dinner service, and take all the necessary steps to make your work food safe (*see* page 94), then restricting the decoration to the edge of the plates away from the cutting area is a sensible precaution, although every day wear and tear will inevitably damage your work and eventually lessen the impact of bringing the plates to the table – so keep them for special occasions. This is the most difficult project in the book, and relies almost solely on free-hand drawing and painting.

MATERIALS AND EQUIPMENT

● *masking tape* ● *pencil* ●
black marker pen ● *compass*
● *ceramic paints* ● *paint
brushes*
· · · · · ·

PREPARATION AND TIPS

● Although the photographs illustrate the stages in decorating a dinner plate, the same techniques equally apply to a plate of any size. Similarly, you can use elements of the design to decorate the rest of your dinner service: perhaps just a cluster of roses about the lid of a soup tureen, or the simple scalloped border around the outside of a bowl.

● Water-based ceramic paints, which are hardened off in a warm oven, will add a degree of permanence to the finished plate, but remember that the result will not then be food safe unless the item is fired.

● The design here is very delicate, and requires skill and patience if you are to achieve a professional finish. You will reduce the risk of smudging freshly-painted details if you paint in a clockwise direction if you are right-handed, and anti-clockwise if you are left-handed.

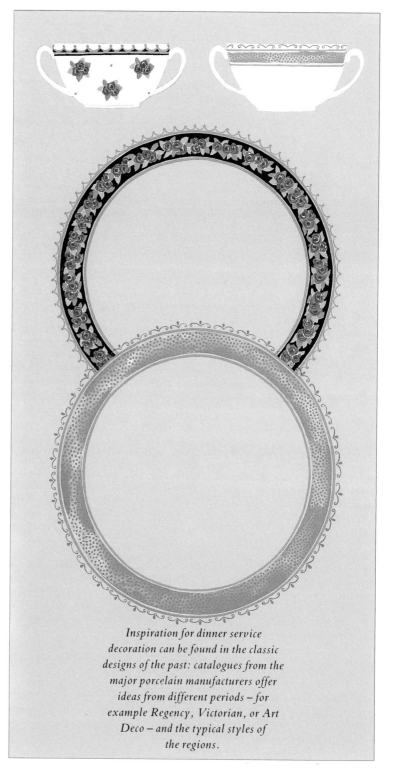

Inspiration for dinner service decoration can be found in the classic designs of the past: catalogues from the major porcelain manufacturers offer ideas from different periods – for example Regency, Victorian, or Art Deco – and the typical styles of the regions.

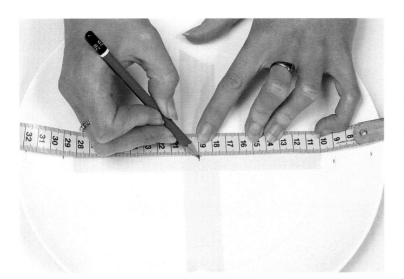

1 Mark out the border area to be painted on the edge of your dinner plate. Stick two strips of masking tape across the middle of the plate to form a cross that finishes at the inside of the rim of the plate. Measure the diameter of the plate from left to right and top to bottom and mark, as accurately as possible, the central point on the masking tape. (The masking tape will prevent your compass from sliding when you come to use it.)

2 Decide on the position of the two ochre circles around the rim of the plate. To some extent, this will depend on the proportions of the plate, and the width of the rim. Here, the outer circle is 1cm (⅜in) from the outer edge of the plate, and the inner circle is 1 cm (⅜in) from the inner edge of the rim. Mark these points at quartile intervals on the edge of the plate – this will enable you to check that the compass correctly describes the two circles you want. Set your compass to the correct diameter, place the point in the masking tape and draw in the outer and then the inner circles.

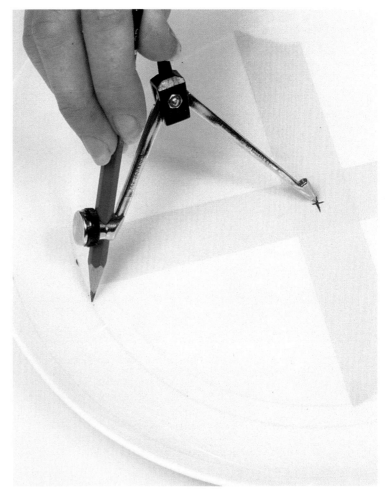

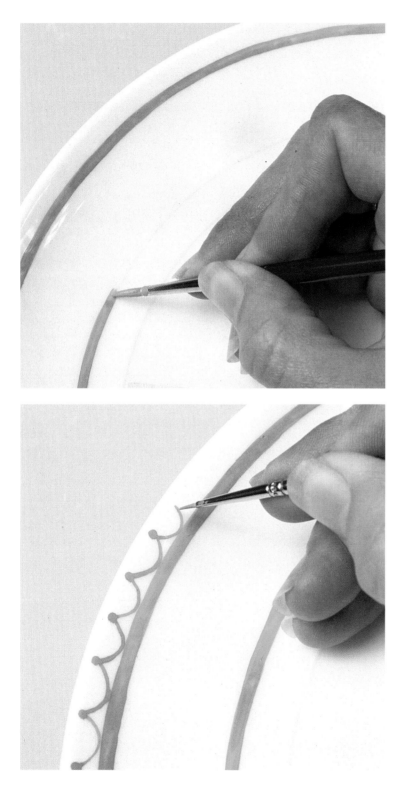

3 Remove the masking tape from the middle of the plate and paint in the two circles using a medium paint brush and ochre paint, and following the two pencil circles as a guide. Paint the outer circle first, then the inner one (your hand will smudge the drying paint of the inner circle if you paint the circles the other way around). Allow the paint to dry.

4 Next, paint the scalloped edge. This is done entirely freehand, using the ochre paint and a fine paint brush – the detail is really too fine to pencil it in first. Paint in four or five of the scallop shapes, then go back and add the small dots at the top points where they meet. Work around the whole of the rim of the plate in this way, then wait for the paint to dry.

DECORATIVE PLATE

5 The plate is now ready for drawing in the clusters of roses. Use a fine black marker pen or a sharp 2B (soft) pencil for this. The rose shapes are only quite rough, and are clustered in groups of three. As you can see, your outline drawings can be quite approximate, but remember to leave sufficient spaces between the groups of flowers for the leaves to be added. Work around the plate until you have filled all the rim with rose clusters.

6 Paint the roses in a pink-red colour. Remember that this should be pale enough to allow you to fill in details in a darker red at a later stage. Use a fine paint brush, and take care not to fill in all of the area representing each flower. Try to achieve a fairly sketchy look, so that some of the white of the plate still shows through, delineating the different flowers and the rose petals. When you have worked round all the flowers, allow the paint to dry.

7 Use the fine black marker pen or the 2B pencil to draw in the leaves around the roses. As with the flowers, these should be done freehand, and you should not seek slavishly to make them all the same; in fact, small variations will add to the overall impact and interest of the decoration.

8 Paint some of the leaves pale green, allow the paint to dry, and then paint the remainder dark green. As far as is possible, try to alternate pale and dark leaves. Leave a thin outline of white plate between the rose petals and the leaves to add to the definition of the design.

9 When the green paint is dry, finish off painting the flowers. Mix a darker red paint, and use the finest paint brush you have to add details: paint a roughly circular shape in the middle, and small sweeps of the brush radiating outwards to give depth and definition. Leave to dry.

10 Finish off by painting the background of the border in black. Using a fine paint brush, paint an outline around the flowers and the leaves and along the edges of the ochre circles, trying to leave a small amount of white showing through. Do this for a small section of the plate, then go back and fill in the rest of the background. Work your way around the plate in this way until you have finished.

KILNS AND FIRING

THE MAIN PURPOSE of this book has been to introduce an exciting new craft to the home hobbyist, and the primary emphasis has therefore been on materials and techniques for projects which can be quickly and cheaply made at home by oven-firing. The only drawback, as has been pointed out, is that these items are then more susceptible to damage than kiln-fired objects, and, although the paints may be described as non-toxic, the finished piece can never be fully food safe unless it is fired at a much higher temperature in a kiln. In any case, if you enjoy making the projects created for this volume, you will inevitably wish to go on to design your own, and to produce objects which have a functional as well as a decorative purpose.

The sensible first step is to learn more about kilns and kiln-firing by approaching a local craft group or friendly professional potter. It is generally easy, and inexpensive, to arrange for some of your work to be fired in their kiln, and by working with them you will learn the basic rules, and could save yourself a great deal of time and money when you come to make your own investment. Get specific advice from the teacher or person handling the kiln about what materials to use and how to present your work: conditions and kiln-types vary, and they may have special requirements.

Buying a ceramic kiln to set up your own studio need not be the massive investment you might expect – but do think carefully about how you will use it and what you really need. The largest kiln that can be run off a domestic electricity supply is about 1.4 cubic feet,

and this can be purchased for around £450 (UK)/$800 (USA). However this is a basic model and would limit your ability to fire several items at once, or to produce larger, or taller, pieces. A larger model – 2.6 cubic feet – would cost around £600/$1100, but will need special adaption to the electricity supply.

There are essentially two methods of firing decorative designs: hard-fire and soft-fire (or muffled firing). Hard-firing is used where the design has been painted on to unfired (raw) glaze, so that the decoration is merged into the base. The required temperature is about 1400°C for porcelain and between 750–1100°C for earthenware. Once the object is fired, the decoration is irrevocably set, and cannot be touched-up or altered. Soft-firing is more relevant to the type of work developed in this book. The design is made on an already glazed piece, and the firing (at 830°C for porcelain or 730°C for earthenware) fixes even the most delicate work with precision.

For soft-firing the decoration is applied with 'vitrifiable' paints, that become hard and glass-like during the process. They are available in various forms – from powders you can mix yourself, to gouache-like paste or pastille – and can be augmented by 'lustres' (special varnishes) and even precious metals such as gold. Colours can change during firing at high temperatures, and it is worth making a test piece, preferably using an identical base material, so you know the resulting shades before investing time in the finished design. All of these materials are available in craft stores or at your local potters' supplies outlet.

PAINTED CERAMICS AS GIFTS

MOST OF THE PROJECTS in the book would make beautiful presents. In addition they could be adapted or personalized by, for example, integrating into the design the recipient's favourite flowers, fruits or animal characters. Once your hand-lettering skills are sufficiently refined, all manner of options are possible, from a simple mug with someone's name on it, to celebratory or commemorative plates or plaques to mark birthdays, christenings, retirements or special occasions.

Do always bear in mind that although you know how much work went into making a beautiful decorative object, the recipient, or someone in their household, or (heaven forbid) at a jumble sale in fifteen years' time, may forget that the piece is purely ornamental and try to use it. Unless you have kiln-fired it, *always* take the precaution of painting on the back "Not food safe or dishwasher-proof". You will probably wish, in any case, to put your name on the back or bottom of the item.

SOURCES

All the materials and equipment in this book – with the exception of ceramic kilns, which are sold by specialist potters' supplies stores – are commonly available in high street art and craft shops, or from the following major manufacturers, distributors and wholesalers:

Potterycrafts Ltd, Harrison Bell, Campbell Road, Stoke-on-Trent, England ST4 4ET. **Tel:0782 74500**

(Potterycrafts Ltd can supply a range of white china 'blanks' and ceramic kilns, as well as the more basic materials discussed. They also organize an extensive network of ceramic painting groups and classes.)

Nationart Inc., 220 Ballardvale Street, Wilmington, MA 01877, USA. Tel: 508 657 5995

Francheville Pty Ltd, 1–5 Perry Street, Collingwood, 3066, Victoria, Australia. Tel: 03 416 0611

Parker Craft Pty Ltd, PO Box 1721, Bedfordview 2008, Johannesburg, South Africa. Tel: 011 453 83 26

Pebeo, Parc d'Activites de Gemenos, Avenue du Pic de Bretagne, BP 106, 13881 Gemenos cedex, France. Tel: 42 32 08 08

Pebeo are distributed in the UK by Art Graphique, Unit 2 Poulton Close, Dover, Kent CT17 0HL. Tel: 304 242244

The Publishers offer their grateful thanks to Potterycrafts Ltd, Pebeo (France), Art Graphique, and Nationart Inc for their extensive help.

INDEX